In Need Of Assistants

Iain Moss began writing at Oxford in the 1970's as a member of the Etceteras, Oxford's equivalent of the Cambridge Footlights. After teaching English as a foreign language in France and Austria, he went on to a successful business career spanning more than 30 years which took him and his family all over the world. He now lives in Malaysia with his wife, two daughters and a dog called Clyde.

I0134681

In Need Of Assistants

Iain Moss

Narra House Publishing

www.narrahouse.com

Published in 2012 by Narra House Publishing
Copyright © 2012 by Iain Moss

ISBN: 978-0-9559892-2-3

To my wife Eunice – the ultimate goal of all my travels

Chapter One

The Tyrolean Express drew slowly into Innsbruck main station and juddered to a halt amid a clicking and a banging of doors that had started well before the train had stopped. The picturesque landscape of forbidding grey mountains had long since given way to the railway-side grimness of station approaches the world over. I should have been excited but I felt like I'd travelled halfway across the world and left somewhere far behind me any spirit of adventure and capacity for excitement I might once have possessed.

It hadn't actually been half the world but it had been a long way. From London via Dover and a sleeping North Sea to Belgium and Germany, then across into Austria, storybook perfect in the cold light of early morning and on to Vienna for our induction course. After three days of warnings and lectures, lost suitcases and strange food, unbreakable bonds of friendship with people I would never see again, it was finally to Innsbruck, dull and dismal in the early winter gloom, our final destination and our home for the next year.

"Well, here we are, impressive isn't it?" said a voice, cutting into my thoughts.

I cast a jaundiced eye round the dirty station buildings and decided Mike was being ironic. It wasn't. Apart from the hoardings advertising skiing equipment we could just as easily have been in Scunthorpe or Luton.

"It's hardly the Innsbruck of the travel brochures," I said. "Where are all the cheery locals in quaint Tyrolean dress slapping their thighs and dancing to oompah bands?"

"At work I should think," said Mike. "After all, it's 12 o'clock on a Thursday morning in October. Not exactly the height of the tourist season."

"No, I suppose not."

"It makes you wonder what we're doing here really, doesn't it?"

"I've been wondering that ever since we left Vienna," I said.

We'd had to leave the hostel in Vienna at dawn, long before

breakfast was served, and then trudge loaded down with our worldly possessions, to the nearest tram stop half-a-mile away. The weather was already bitterly cold and the streets were thick with copper coloured leaves blown from the trees in the adjacent park. Numb, wind-sore faces and the sombre half-light had contributed to our already growing feeling of gloom and we had completed most of the slow, meandering tram journey to Vienna main station in silence. From there it had been five long hours on the train to Innsbruck, across three-quarters of Austria, through scenery varying from the banal to the magnificent. But the forests, lakes and mountains had struck no chord in us at all.

Mike and I had come to Austria as 'exchange assistants' - language students brought over to teach English in Austrian schools while Austrian students went over to England to teach German. And a very good arrangement it was too. We learned German properly while living and working among native German speakers and Austrian children had the benefit of conversation and personal contact with real English people, hopefully thereby adding a new dimension to their studies. It wasn't just limited to Austria either. All over Europe thousands of students were taking part in the same kind of exchange, bartering their own language and culture in order to learn and experience someone else's. I wondered whether they were undergoing a sudden spirit of adventure deficiency as well.

"Well, like it or not, we've arrived," said Mike. "What do we do now?"

"We could try panicking for a bit, see if that helps," I suggested helpfully.

"True, we could do that. But I was thinking of something a bit more positive."

We both thought quietly for a few moments, desperately trying to come up with something constructive.

"Right, got it," said Mike, at last, with the air of a man determined to keep his head when all around him were losing theirs, "positive action."

He began to tick off points on his fingers as he spoke. "Firstly, we haven't got a clue where we're staying because our schools didn't bother to reply to our letters. Secondly, neither of us knows Innsbruck so we haven't a clue how far our schools are from here or in which direction. Thirdly, we've........

"I thought this was supposed to be positive," I interrupted.

"Hang on, hang on, I'm getting there." He went back to counting on his fingers. "Thirdly, we've both got far too much luggage to go dragging it round a strange town. So why don't we dump our cases in 'left luggage' and buy a map of Innsbruck. If the schools are close we can walk there, present ourselves for duty and ask for somewhere to live, otherwise we can share a taxi."

He looked at me proudly, the man with the solution.

"Alright," I conceded, "that's positive."

"And then we can panic later."

"You've just spoiled it," I said.

We picked up our luggage and wandered over to the left luggage office, situated, for some unknown reason, just outside the main station complex. I let Mike do most of the talking since he'd spent long periods in Germany and spoke German almost fluently already. My spoken German was pitiful as befitted the product of 'A' level German and two years studying languages at an English University. Obviously, in the long run I had that much more to gain than Mike so it wasn't too much of a drawback, but I couldn't help feeling a certain amount of envy as I watched him skilfully conduct his negotiations with the man behind the counter. Then I gratefully exchanged my suitcase, holdall and carrier bags for a slip of pink paper and we moved on.

"OK," said Mike, "step two. Let's buy a map."

"I've got a better idea," I said. "Let's find a tourist office and get one for nothing."

In the event, however, my one positive contribution of the morning proved to be unnecessary. As we were preparing to go off in search of a map, somebody behind us suddenly called our names. In a foreign town where we didn't know a soul this was unexpected to say the least and we both wheeled round in surprise. Over in the station car park, a girl was waving at us from the window of a bright orange VW Beetle.

"Should have guessed," exclaimed Mike, a delighted grin on his face. "It's Jane."

Jane had been one of the people we'd met in Vienna. As part of the induction course people who were to be based in the same town or region were introduced and given an opportunity to get to know each other. We weren't actively encouraged to spend too much time together during the year in case it interfered with our learning of German, but it was seen as a useful safety net if we had problems, needed help, or simply wanted someone to talk to. The first person I'd met, in fact, had been Mike and we'd been clinging to each other for support ever since.

We hadn't really expected to see much of Jane. She had already spent a year in Innsbruck studying at the University as part of her degree course. She'd returned to England to do her final year and then requested this posting to come back and be with her Austrian boyfriend whom she planned to marry. Even if we only saw her this once, she couldn't have picked a better time.

"Hello there," she said chirpily, as we walked over to the car. "Want a lift?"

"God, you're a wonderful sight," I said, meaning every word.

"That's what he thinks, too," she replied, pointing at the small bearded man in the driving seat. "This is Gerhard my boyfriend."

Gerhard spoke very little English and just nodded politely as Jane did the introductions.

"Gerhard's an engineer," she said, "or at least he will be on Monday. That's when he starts work after six years of idleness at the University." She translated this for Gerhardt's benefit who feigned indignation before laughing and giving her a playful tap on the leg.

"How on earth did you know when to meet us?" Mike asked, apparently suspecting clairvoyance of some kind.

"Well it wasn't difficult to guess, was it? I knew you were coming today and that you'd want to get to your schools before they closed after lunch, so you had to be on the early morning express. Elementary my dear Michael." She looked at her watch. "Which reminds me," she continued, "if you still want to get there before they close, we'd better get a move on."

Jane got out of the car and pulled down the front seat to let us into the back.

"Right then," she said, climbing back in and fastening her seatbelt.

"Where to?"

We gave her the names and addresses of our schools and she had a brief conversation with Gerhardt.

"Apparently yours is the furthest away," she said to me, "so we'll drop you first, OK?"

"Fine," I answered, not feeling fine at all.

Gerhardt put the little Volkswagen in gear and set off down the street behind a slow-moving red and white tram.

There was little improvement in the scenery as we drove along, just the same old shops and grimy buildings. But by then I'd rather lost interest in my surroundings anyway. The awful reality of the situation was just beginning to hit me properly. It had been easy to ignore the difficulties back in July, in England, when I'd accepted the post and concentrate only on the skiing and the adventure of being abroad for a year. With a posting like Innsbruck, it had been great fun watching the look of envy in people's eyes when I'd told them where I was going. Even in Vienna it had still seemed a long way off and I'd managed to push the worst of my fears to the back of my mind. Now it was all happening for real - a year in a foreign country away from my family and friends teaching in a foreign school, and I couldn't hide behind the glamorous fantasy any longer. Of course what it needed was a bit of backbone, strength of character, stiff upper lip. All I seemed to be able to summon up at that precise moment was a queasy stomach and a full bladder. The worst thing of all was that I knew that, even if I hated every minute of it, I would have to stay the full year. My tutors would not be at all amused if I came running back half way through. Innsbruck was a prestige post and if I walked out before the end it would seriously affect candidates from my college in future years.

All too soon we drew up outside a large, relatively modern building in its own grounds set back from the road.

"Well this is it," said Jane, turning round in her seat, "the *Bundesrealgymnasium.* This is where you get off."

I was a bit taken aback at first. For some reason, I'd pictured the school as being much older, all red brick and corridors smelling of disinfectant and boiled cabbage, just like my own school in England. It was totally illogical, in fact, because, if I'd thought about it sensibly, I would have realised immediately that it was almost guaranteed to be modern. It was a relatively new idea, the *Bundesrealgymnasium*, specialising in a more contemporary scientific and technical education rather than the traditional classical and literary education offered by a *Bundesgymnasium*. I was beginning to realise that there was quite a lot about living in Austria that I hadn't given any sensible thought to. Still this time it was a pleasant surprise because the school was new, bright and clean and, superficially at least, not a bad place to spend a year. Jane climbed out of the car and pulled back the seat for me. As I clumsily manoeuvred my way past the seat and out of the narrow door, I touched Mike on the arm.

"Good luck, Mike," I said, "I hope you get a warm welcome at your school."

"And you too. Look, why don't we meet up again later and swap notes?"

I was secretly greatly relieved at this suggestion. I was already beginning to feel quite pathetically lonely, even before they'd left.

"Where's a good place to meet, Jane?" I asked.

She thought about it for a few moments.

"I suppose Moby Dick's is as good a place as any. It's tucked away between the station and the main street. I know everyone always says 'you can't miss it' but really you can't. And anyway everyone knows it, so just ask if you get lost."

"What time, then?" said Mike.

Jane thought again. "Well, if we make it about three that should give both of you plenty of time to finish whatever you have to do."

"Ok, fine," I said. "I'll see you all there at three."

I waited as Jane got back into the car and then waved as the Beetle moved off and disappeared round the corner. This was it. I was all on my own now. I took a few moments to compose myself and give the butterflies in my stomach a chance to die down. There was one phrase in German I had to be able to produce word perfect, or at least intelligibly, and that was 'I am the new English assistant.' As I forced myself to walk towards the school entrance, I began to repeat the phrase over and over to myself like some Hindu mantra designed to bring me great spiritual peace. I was still chanting quietly to myself as I entered the building and came across a little wizened man in a blue overall sitting on an old wooden chair by the door. I guessed correctly that he must be the caretaker.

"Good Morning," I said, taking my courage in both trembling hands, "I'm the new English assistant."

I don't know whether it was my accent, pronunciation or simply the unexpectedness of my appearance but all the practice had been a waste of time. He just looked at me blankly and said: "Sorry?"

I tried again, more slowly this time, emphasizing each word, and a glimmer of understanding appeared on his face.

"Ah," he said, smiling broadly, "English, yes?"

"Yes, that's right. I'm an English teacher." I searched my mind desperately for some more vocabulary. "I want to see the Headmaster."

He looked at me sorrowfully. "The Headmaster's not here today."

"Could I see another English teacher?"

He looked even more crestfallen.

"There are none here today."

"Is there anybody here?"

"No. They're all out walking. It's a *Wandertag*."

I hadn't the first idea what a *Wandertag* was but it didn't matter much. The main point was that nobody was there and that was a catastrophe.

"Will they be back tomorrow?"

"Yes, yes," he said, visibly relieved to be able to help at last, "everyone will be here tomorrow."

There wasn't much more I could do.

"I'll come back tomorrow, then," I said. "Thank you for your help."

"It's a pleasure, *Herr Professor*."

Herr Professor was a courtesy title reserved for teachers in status conscious Austria but I was too preoccupied to be flattered. Quite apart from being annoyed that nobody had bothered to be there to meet me, I was in a proper mess now and I didn't really have a clue what I was going to do next.

I left the school and walked back out onto the main road. There was an empty bus shelter there with a bench so I sat down for a while to try and sort things out in my mind. All in all, I was worse off than when I'd left Vienna. At least before I'd had the comforting illusion that once I arrived and announced myself to a Headmaster, desperate for me to come and revolutionise the teaching of English in his school, he'd look after me like some long lost prodigal son. I was now beginning to have a sneaking suspicion that life just wasn't like that. They either weren't expecting me or, more likely, my arrival wasn't the earth-shattering event in the life of the school that Vienna had hinted it would be.

I was starting to feel fairly certain that nobody would have thought about where I was going to live. Whatever happened, I was going to have to find somewhere temporary for at least one night and probably more. It was a selfish thought but part of me hoped that Mike was having similar problems at his school, then at least I wouldn't have to do it all on my own. My already poor opinion of my German had sunk even lower in the past ten minutes and, as if it wasn't bad enough already, I was going to have to cope with the Tyrolean accent and dialect as well. I'd studied German at a very traditional English University where literature and prose translation were seen as the main ingredients of a language degree. There had been the occasional conversation class, almost as an afterthought, but real spoken proficiency was neither thought necessary nor encouraged. I was certainly not equipped to handle the version of German spoken around Innsbruck. It was like the German equivalent of Geordie and I was going to have exactly the same kind of problems as a foreign English student going to live in Newcastle. It was a daunting prospect and I knew I was going to have to rely heavily on Mike for a while until I managed to develop some fluency and, more importantly, enough confidence to trust my own command of the language.

My fleeting visit to the school had left me with hours to kill before I could meet up with the others again and since there didn't seem much point in loitering in a bus shelter, I decided to head back towards the town centre and have a look round. The area around the school, now that I looked at it properly, was actually rather pleasant. Not that it was especially scenic, just quiet peaceful suburbia untainted by the grime from the railway I'd seen everywhere else en route. There were trees lining the streets, very little traffic on the roads and a handful of small local shops, including a bank and a coffee shop along the main road opposite the school. What set it apart from an English city suburb, however, dominating the view in every direction, were the mountains, the main reason I'd chosen Innsbruck in the first place. As yet no snow had fallen and they were grey and brown and bare but I knew that by mid-December they would be clean and white under a blanket of new snow. I'd only ever skied once before, in a tiny resort in France, sleeping on a friend's hard wooden floor at night and learning to ski by trial and error on my own during the day. It wasn't exactly a glamorous introduction to the sport but I'd loved it all the same and come to the Austrian Tyrol for a year, as opposed to any of the thousands of other places I could have chosen, solely on the strength of it. I was beginning to wonder now if that had actually been a logical way of deciding where to spend a year of my life.

I'd already begun to realise that I was totally ignorant about the country I'd come to live in. The induction course in Vienna had been very useful in providing some basic facts of life. We had attended formal lectures on the Austrian education system, and had had a superficial introduction to the teaching of English to German speakers. We had been told what we could and could not do in school and what we should avoid doing out of school. But as for politics, social structures, local customs and everything else, these we had to learn as we went along. Since I'd left England knowing only that they spoke German, the men wore funny leather shorts and that you could ski there, I had rather a long way to go. However, it was a trifle late to do anything about it at this stage so I pushed the thought away in favour of my more pressing problems and set off towards town.

Chapter Two

As predicted I found Moby Dick's without too much trouble tucked away in a small square between the station and Maria-Theresien-Strasse, the main street. It turned out to be a new, modern, plastic affair, one of a chain of restaurants around Innsbruck. It was full of naval memorabilia, oddly out of place among the modern seats and tables, and the Gents toilet bore the legend 'Captains.' I've always had a deep mistrust of places which give their toilets twee names and that, coupled with a menu consisting entirely of expensive hamburgers and pseudo Italian food, convinced me that this was one place that I wouldn't be spending much time in over the year. Its one saving grace was a charming little piazza outside with trees in tubs and neatly arranged flower beds and I guessed that this is why Jane had chosen it. It was only later that I found out that the building on the other side of the piazza housed the English faculty of the University making 'Moby's' a popular rendezvous among the students. At the time it held no interest for me at all and once I'd made sure I could find my way back to it later, I moved on.

It felt strange actually to be in Innsbruck after so many months of anticipation. In fact, it was only now, as I approached the centre, that it really began to register that I was there at all. Virtually everything of interest in Innsbruck lay in the small area bounded by the railway on one side and the river on the other. Outside of that lay suburbia like suburbia anywhere in Northern Europe. It was a pity I hadn't got things sorted out at my school and, indeed, in my own mind, because it should have been a wonderful feeling walking through those streets for the first time. Here I was at twenty-one on the threshold of spending a year in one of the most beautiful towns in Europe - a year of minimal responsibility and maximum opportunity - and all I could do was wish I was back home safe and sound in England.

Although ill-prepared in almost every other way possible, I had read several guide books on Innsbruck before coming here and formed an impression of how the town would look. They'd all gone into raptures about the main street, Maria-Theresien-Strasse, and the surrounding area. In fact, most of the key 'sights' seemed to be in the main street or at either end almost as if it had been designed for the benefit of the tour guides. From past experience, I had learned to be very wary about travel writers and take a lot of their enthusiasm with a pinch of salt. I'd been disappointed before by views described as breathtaking and buildings cited as examples of architectural splendour. Part of the problem was the 'Blue Danube' syndrome - what you see depends to a large extent on what kind of mood you are in at the time. This time, however, I was pleasantly surprised and considering, I wasn't in the best of moods for sightseeing, it says a lot for the area that I found it every bit as impressive as I'd been led to expect.

I entered Maria-Theresien-Strasse from a side road, turning to face north and there ahead of me was the Old Town set against the panorama of the *Nordkette* chain of the Alps. The lovely old Gothic buildings with their arcades and large bay windows looked like something from a Grimm fairy-tale and the magical effect was enhanced by the sunlight glinting off the golden roof of one of the buildings in the centre. This was obviously the famous *Goldenes Dachl*. I was delighted, not least because this was Austria as I had imagined it should be. Up until now I had been disappointed by the houses and buildings around the town, looking so much like those in any town in England, but now anticipation was rewarded. I was reminded forcibly of a description I had read somewhere - 'Innsbruck, where the mountains stand half into the sky at the end of every street.' And so it was, not town surrounded by mountains but mountains as an integral part of the architecture of the town.

The Old Town itself was made up of a network of narrow, winding, cobbled streets leading down towards the river Inn. It was heavily populated with restaurants, coffee shops, old-fashioned Booksellers vying with each other to have the largest, most ostentatious sign and the inevitable souvenir shops. It amazed me that so many could survive in such close proximity to each other, especially as they offered, by and large, the same range of souvenirs. The tourist trade was obviously phenomenal during the season. I guessed that it was also probably a long season. There would be skiers all through the winter and climbers, walkers and general tourists through the late spring and summer. In fact, there were probably tourists there right through the year. This was another thing I hadn't given much thought to before coming but it was potentially a big problem. Most people associated with the tourist trade were likely to speak English, which might make it difficult for me to practise my German and there was also the danger that I would be treated as just another tourist throughout the year and never really become accepted as someone who lived and worked there. But there was always that risk when you chose to come and work in a big town. It was the price you paid for living somewhere with lots to do. The opposite extreme was the small village where nobody spoke English, apart from the teachers at the school and your pupils, and everyone knew who you were. If you were accepted by the community it was an unequalled opportunity to learn the language and experience their way of life. If not, it could be a year of purgatory.

The smell of the cheeses and hams, which hit me every time I walked past a grocer's shop and the beckoning aroma of fresh ground coffee were beginning to sap my will. The window displays of the coffee houses were a forty days and forty nights of temptation to the figure conscious and the tables which had spilled out into the square in front of the *Goldenes Dachl* were packed with old ladies in their Loden suits with the embroidered collars and Tirolean hats impaled on ornate feather stick-pins who had clearly given up the struggle years before.

I'd discovered in Vienna that coffee houses are the churches in which coffee is worshipped. In those days, long before Starbucks came along, for example, Austria already had twelve different classifications of coffee depending on strength and the proportion of milk. One of the first things you learn when studying languages is that the Eskimos have an astonishing number of words for snow. Nobody ever tells you that the Austrians have twelve words for coffee. These range from *Melange*, a weak blend served half and half with hot milk, through to *Mokka*, strong and black and usually heavily sweetened. The coffee house itself has all the calm and gentility of a gentleman's club. Newspapers attached to wooden batons are there for your pleasure along with a selection of national and international magazines and glasses of iced water are discreetly placed at your elbow at regular intervals lest thirst interfere with your relaxation. They are a place to sit and watch the world pass by as you say goodbye to any last vestige of a firm, flat stomach. As I threaded my way through the tables I looked with growing greed on the coffee and hot chocolate suffocating under fluffy pillows of whipped cream, the plump strudel oozing fruit and nuts, the glistening *Sachertorte*, a chocolate delight glazed with even more chocolate and finally gave up the struggle myself. I sat down at an empty table, reached for a magazine and called the waiter.

Around three I made my way back to Moby Dick's to meet the others. As I approached across the piazza my heart sank. Sitting outside at a table were Jane and Gerhardt but there was no sign of Mike at all. I knew that Gerhardt spoke no English and I had no confidence whatsoever in my German. I desperately wanted to pour out the whole story about what had happened at the school and get some advice on what to do next and I was going to have trouble doing it in German. But that was why I was here after all and I was going to have to get used to it like it or not. As I reached the table Gerhardt smiled and said:

"Want a beer?"

"I'd love one, thanks."

He signalled to the waiter and ordered three more beers.

"Well," asked Jane in German, "how did you get on then? All fixed up?"

"Not exactly no."

"Oh, what happened?"

Painfully, in faltering and largely ungrammatical German, I started to tell them what had happened. After a couple of sentences Jane recognized that it was going to take all day like this and turned to Gerhardt.

"Do you mind if we speak English for a little while, darling?" she said.

Gerhardt smiled and waved me to continue and with a sigh of relief I proceeded to tell her the whole story, pouring out my confusion and frustration about what had happened at the school.

"And so you see," I concluded at last, "I doubt whether they've found me anywhere to live, I don't even know whether they're expecting me at all, and I certainly haven't got anywhere to stay tonight. It's all a bit much."

She smiled sympathetically.

"I understand why you're upset but you really mustn't let it get to you. It's just bad luck that you turned up today of all days. They have these *Wandertags* about six times a year. Every school does it. Each teacher takes his class out for the day for a ramble in the country or a cultural visit somewhere. The dates are fixed at the beginning of the year. They didn't go today just to spite you."

"I gathered that, but you would have thought that someone would have stayed behind to meet me. The head English teacher, for example."

Jane shrugged her shoulders.

"Well personally, I don't think for one moment that they did know you were coming today. I suspect that all they get from the Ministry is confirmation that you've accepted the post and that you'll be here ready to start by Monday. I mean, realistically speaking, the arrival of the English assistant isn't exactly the highlight of the school term. The English department will be glad to have you but I'm sure the Headmaster doesn't really care whether you turn up or not."

"Oh good," I said, "that makes me feel much better."

Jane laughed.

"Come on," she said, "it's not as bad as all that. You're still their responsibility. They can't leave you to sleep under newspapers in the park."

"Except tonight," I said ironically. "Mind you, I could always go and expose myself in the park. That might solve the accommodation problem for a while."

"Might make teaching a bit difficult, though. They'd have a job getting thirty children into a prison cell."

"Well, since they don't seem to care much whether I'm there to teach or not it might solve their problem," I said morosely.

Jane looked at me mockingly.

"Oh how bitter and twisted!"

It was my turn to laugh.

"Alright," I agreed, "I'm taking this too personally. But tonight is a problem. What am I going to do?"

"It's not insurmountable. If it's just you, you can come and sleep on our floor. If Mike's in the same boat then I recommend you get a room in one of the inns in the Old Town. It works out reasonably cheap for two people sharing and our flat's a bit small for two of you. And anyway we're quite a way outside town and you'd be better off in the centre." She gave me a motherly pat on the head. "Now cheer up and drink your beer before it gets warm."

Not long afterwards Mike arrived looking very much like I'd felt earlier in the day.

"Oh God," he said, slumping down on a chair, "I need a beer."

Gerhardt obligingly ordered another round.

"You look worse than Iain," said Jane. "What on earth have they done to you?"

"Not a lot", said Mike with feeling, "just sent me on wild bloody goose chases all over town and generally acted like they'd rather I hadn't bothered to turn up."

His beer arrived and, clutching it to him like his life depended on it, he filled us in on the day's events.

Although his school hadn't disappeared off into the countryside, it was the Head of Department's day off. Nobody else seemed to have any idea what to do with him and they had tried to send him away until tomorrow. However, Mike had insisted and in the end, he had been taken to see the Headmaster. When questioned the Headmaster had disclaimed all knowledge of Mike's letter and eventually, presumably just to get rid of him, he'd pointed out that part of Mike's time would be spent working at the Technical Academy and suggested Mike go and talk to the staff there and see what they'd arranged. So Mike had trekked all the way across town only to find that the Head of the English Department had already gone home for the day and, inevitably, nobody else was expecting him.

"But what really got to me most," said Mike, finally, "was that just as I was leaving the first school, I saw my letter asking for accommodation pinned on the notice board in the staffroom. There was a covering note asking anyone who could help to sign below and, of course, it was empty. So I know full well that they haven't found me anywhere to live. How about you?" he asked, turning to me. "Did you get fixed up OK?"

I filled him in briefly on my lightening visit.

"Well at least that's not quite so bad. There's still a chance they might have found you somewhere."

"I doubt it somehow. I'm beginning to suspect it's not something they bother to do. Anyhow we still have to find somewhere to sleep tonight. Jane suggests a hotel."

"Anywhere in particular Jane?" asked Mike. "You know a convenient Salvation Army hostel or whatever they have here?"

"I don't think you need to sink quite that low just yet. *Der Goldene Löwe* is probably your best bet. It's cheap and it's clean and the restaurant's not bad. Anyway it'll be good experience for you - a night in a real old-fashioned Tyrolean inn."

"It's an experience I'd rather have missed on my first night, thank you very much," said Mike, morosely.

"Well you might not realise it yet but you're both actually very lucky. At least your schools are in town. Mine's way outside."

I suddenly felt rather guilty. I had been so wrapped up in my own problems I'd not even thought to ask Jane how she'd got on at her school.

"Did you get sorted out alright at your place?" I asked.

"Well I went first thing this morning, after driving down last night, and managed to catch my Head of Department before class. He was a bit surprised to see me so soon but I was expected sometime around now. He's given me a timetable and I start work on Monday. Actually, it's rather ironic really..."

She stopped and smiled sheepishly.

"Why?"

"They'd actually found me a place to live but of course I don't need it."

Mike perked up at this.

"Well that's alright, one of us can have it instead. That would at least solve one problem."

Jane shook her head. "It wouldn't be any good to either of you, I'm afraid," she said. "It's miles away, right near my school."

Mike lost interest again.

"Why is it that your school took the trouble to find you accommodation and Mike's didn't?" I asked. "Especially as I presume you didn't write and ask them to."

"You're both the wrong sex, I'm afraid," said Jane with a wry smile. "The Austrians would never dream of leaving a girl without somewhere safe to live, whereas men can look after themselves. I mean we girls have our virginity to protect."

"Oh, I see," said Mike, "and you're living with Gerhardt here to protect your virginity?"

Jane blushed and laughed.

"Not exactly, no. Anyway the accommodation they'd arranged for me was a room in a house owned by an old widow, with all meals provided. Hardly your scene I should think."

"No definitely not," I said with feeling. "Maybe I'd rather find my own accommodation after all."

Der Goldene Löwe stood gloomy and depressing on the corner of one of the narrow cobbled streets in the Old Town. It was only distinguished from all the other old, dark, gloomy buildings around it by the huge gold-coloured lion dangling above the entrance. Inside it was dark and dingy and I hoped we wouldn't be staying there too long. The old lady behind the reception desk was friendly, however, and greeted us with a cheery *Grüss Gott, Meine Herren*. Mike, as usual, took control.

"We'd like a double room, with two beds, initially for one night but maybe for more. Would that be possible?"

"Of course, sir," replied the old lady, "that's no problem at all. It will be 300 schillings a night, payable in advance, and you can let me know in the morning if you require a second night. We're not busy at this time of year."

We handed over the money and took our key. Three hundred schillings - about ten pounds in those pre-Euro days - was not excessive by any means but still enough to cause me serious financial difficulties if it went on for more than a few days. I hoped fervently that, despite my sex, my school had made the effort to find me somewhere to live.

We'd picked up our cases from the left luggage office on the way to the hotel and, once the formalities of registering were out of the way, we went and fetched them from Jane's car and dragged them into the foyer.

"Right," announced Jane, "if you're both sorted out, Gerhardt and I will get going. We're having dinner with his parents tonight and we need to freshen up first."

We both thanked them fervently for all their help.

"When we're all settled," said Mike, "we'll take you out for a slap-up meal somewhere."

"Absolutely," I agreed.

"I'll hold you to that. We're actually going away for the weekend tomorrow, to make use of the three days before we start work, but get in touch next week sometime and let us know how you're getting on. I've written our telephone number down for you somewhere." She fumbled in her handbag for a while and finally produced a scrap of paper with the number on it. "Here it is. Ring us next week, okay?"

"We'll do that" said Mike.

The room was at the top of a long, winding staircase. It was drab, cold and functional and the amenities consisted entirely of two beds, a sink and an enormous rickety wardrobe.

Mike and I looked at each other.

"Wonderful," he moaned, sitting down heavily on the nearest bed, "the perfect end to a perfect day. I just can't wait to see what delights tomorrow brings."

I sank down next to him.

"I really don't think I want to know," I said.

Chapter Three

I woke up very early the next morning feeling like nothing on earth. Both Mike and I had slept very badly following a heavy meal in the restaurant and a good deal more local beer than was good for us. After a few hours of alcohol induced stupor we had woken up at different times with raging thirsts and all the discomforts associated with falling asleep fully clothed. I was already feeling the first symptoms of a hangover when I undressed and got into bed and my problems were added to by the unbelievably uncomfortable continental quilt the hotel supplied. It was the thickest quilt I had ever seen and rapidly turned the bed into an oven. It was too cold to sleep without a cover so I spent most of the night tossing and turning in a desperate attempt to get comfortable, while the sweat poured off me. I could hear Mike having similar problems, groaning with frustration at one point and throwing the quilt onto the floor. In the end, he seemed to manage to fall asleep while I dozed fitfully until about six-thirty and then gave up.

That, of course, didn't really solve any problems. My hangover had, by now, reached its climax and I had a headache over one eye. My stomach, fortunately, didn't feel too bad, considering the things I'd forced it to cope with the evening before and I presumed I owed that to the vast quantities of water I'd consumed during the night. I felt like getting up but the last thing I wanted to do was disturb Mike now he was managing to sleep. The sensible thing was to stay there and keep quiet.

For a while, I tried to concentrate on making my headache go away, with a certain amount of success. Unfortunately, as soon as my concentration lapsed, the headache came back again and in the end I gave up. I decided to plan out what I was going to do that day but the prospect of all the problems I was likely to have to face made me feel so much worse that I had to stop that too. After about fifteen minutes I couldn't stand it any longer. Mike or no Mike I had to get up and go out to get some fresh air. As quietly as I could I slipped out from under the quilt and braced myself against the freezing cold. Then, clenching my teeth tightly together, I pulled on the warmest clothes I could find in the case I'd already opened, quietly opened the door of the room and tiptoed outside.

As I wandered down the winding staircase to the ground floor, I could hear the sound of voices and the clatter of cups and plates in the restaurant. They were presumably getting ready to serve breakfast and, since it was included in the price of the room, I hoped I'd be able to force something down later. The more I could put away at breakfast, the less of my dwindling resources I'd have to spend on lunch. With any luck, a walk in the fresh air would clear my head, sharpen my appetite and save me money as well.

Outside it was just getting light and without the sunshine the air was bitterly cold. There was very little activity around the Old Town. The only places open were the bakeries, ready to supply fresh bread to the hotels and restaurants. I wasn't very interested in food at that moment, so I headed down towards the river. The name Innsbruck means, literally, the bridge over the river Inn and I felt that I ought to mark my arrival by crossing the bridge from which it derives its name. This was primarily a safety measure for when I returned to England. Three years previously I'd spent some time in the South of France, not far from Avignon. For some reason, although I'd been to Avignon lots of times, I'd never actually been on the bridge there as commemorated in the song *Sur le pont d'Avignon*. Unfortunately, about the only thing that people in England know about Avignon is that it's got a bridge upon which its inhabitants are given to dancing at regular intervals. Whenever, back in England again, I talked about my stay in France, near Avignon, I was always asked, with monotonous regularity: "Oh, really, did you go on the bridge?" I got so fed up with the looks of disbelief when I answered, shamefacedly, that in fact I hadn't, that this time I was determined to do all the normal touristy things just once so that people would actually believe I'd been there. Should anyone happen to know about the bridge in Innsbruck, I wanted to be able to say with complete conviction that I'd crossed over it and in circumstances which I was likely to remember, such as now. "Oh, you were in Innsbruck?" they might say. "Did you see the bridge from which it derives its name?" "Oh, indeed," I would answer. "I remember crossing it one autumn morning just as dawn was breaking. There was a pale glow over the mountains and the birds...." I wasn't going to be caught out twice.

Actually, I hated sightseeing for the sake of sightseeing. I'd been through the phase of going abroad with a checklist of items to be seen at all costs, rushing around ticking them off madly with no real enjoyment. The main point of the trip seemed to be what you could tell people you'd seen when you got home. My idea of hell now was an eternal InterRail pass, visiting all the great stations of Europe. I had never understood how anybody could get off at Munich or Cologne, wander around the town for a few hours and then claim to have seen Germany. Having said that, I was quite willing to indulge in a little hypocrisy if it made life easier when I got home.

Crossing the bridge, however, was by no means a waste of time. On the other side of the river stood another old quarter of town known as Mariahilf and while its own buildings and winding streets were interesting in their own right, the view back across the river of the Old Town dominated by the City dome and the dual spires of the Cathedral was even better. From there also I could see the rounded summit of the giant Patscherkofel Mountain in the south, scene of Klammer's great triumph for Austria in the Olympic downhill race, and the ski-jump platform soaring down on the Bergisel below the village of Igls. The Innsbrucker to a man were inordinately proud of the fact that Innsbruck had twice played host to the Winter Olympics and there were reminders everywhere. At that time, 1976 in particular was still very clear in everyone's mind and the name Franz Klammer was still guaranteed to evoke sighs of rapture and glazed faraway looks. Officials of the town such as the Mayor were inclined to wax lyrical about Innsbruck's role in nurturing a feeling of unity among the peoples of the world and the bridge as the symbol of that unity was exploited to the full. It was all a little pompous and self important but standing there that morning, looking back across the river Inn, I had to admit that they had every right to be proud of their town. I would only find out with time whether it really promoted unity with foreigners or not!

The walk did me the power of good and I was feeling a lot better by the time I returned to the hotel. I still wasn't particularly hungry but at least now I could make an attempt at breakfast. Mike was up and dressed when I got back and judging by his appearance his powers of recovery were a good deal better than mine.

"Morning," he said brightly, as I walked in. "Where have you been?"

"Walking off a hangover," I replied. "Anyway I couldn't sleep in these beds."

"Weren't the quilts awful? I thought I was never going to get comfortable. It must be an ancient Austrian torture reserved for foreigners."

"Well there's no way I fancy spending another night under one. I just hope to God the schools have sorted something out."

"To be honest, I don't think we're going to have much choice. We're supposed to be out of here by eleven luggage and all and we ought really to be at school by eight, when they start, if only for form's sake. That means we haven't got time to go and dump our things back in left luggage. I don't know about you but I have no intention of lugging my cases around with me all day."

"You think we should book in for another night, don't you?"

"Well, I don't fancy it much but at least that way we don't have to worry about where we're going to sleep tonight and we can leave our things here all day. And anyway, even if our schools have found us somewhere, we won't necessarily be able to move in immediately. I think it's the best bet all round."

I had to concede that he was right even though the prospect was hardly attractive.

After breakfast, a typical Teutonic affair consisting of rolls, jam, sausage and cheese, we paid in advance for a second night and then set off to try our luck again at our schools. For part of the way, we walked together since Mike's school was en route to mine, then we parted company near the town museum.

"By the way," said Mike, as he turned to go, "remember we need to register with the British Consul today. We might as well meet up and do it together."

"OK. What time?"

"I don't know. What time do you think we'll be finished?"

"Well, I shouldn't think they'll keep us much later than three. The schools must close around then. Why don't we meet at four just to play safe?"

"Alright then, I'll see you there at four. Good luck."

"Thanks. And you. I'll see you later."

I'd taken the precaution of picking up a street map at the local tourist office and worked out a more direct route to my school. Before long I came out in the street opposite the school, not far from the bank and the coffee shop. I stopped for a moment to try and summon up all my dwindling courage, without much success, and then crossed the road and went inside.

Inevitably, the first person I met as I went through the door was the caretaker, sitting on his chair by the entrance as if he hadn't moved since the previous day. He gave me a big smile as he saw me.

"Grüss Gott, *Herr Professor*, everyone is here today," he announced cheerfully, obviously pleased that I hadn't taken umbrage and gone straight back to England. "Just go right on up the stairs and you'll find the staffroom at the end of the corridor."

I thanked him politely and climbed the stairs to the first floor. I was slightly surprised by how quiet the school was. I'd expected to find the corridors full of milling children on their way to their first class of the day but everywhere was deserted. It was only just on eight o'clock but it looked as if lessons had already started.

At the top of the stairs, I found a miniature signpost with arrows pointing to the gymnasium, the music room, the science labs and, away to the left, the staffroom and the Headmaster's study. I wasn't really sure where I should present myself, but knowing the Austrians' love of formality and authority it seemed like a good idea to see the Headmaster first. Conscious of the butterflies in my stomach which, over the last few days had become close friends, I found his office and, after a pause for a few deep breaths, I knocked on the door.

I was slightly surprised when a female voice told me to come inside and wondered if maybe I'd misread the sign and was going to meet a Headmistress not a Headmaster. The lady in question turned out, however, to be his secretary, a prim, bespectacled figure with grey hair firmly fixed in a bun. She looked at me disapprovingly over her glasses.

"Yes?" she said, sharply. "Why aren't you in class?"

"Er, um, I'm the new English assistant. I've come to see the Headmaster."

She obviously wasn't expecting this.

"Oh, er, excuse me *Herr Professor*. I thought you were...I mean...er, we weren't...er, we didn't..." she floundered.

I guessed she'd mistaken me for one of the older pupils and that a new English assistant didn't feature anywhere on her schedule for the day. She recovered quickly, however.

"If you could just take a seat for a few moments," she said, resuming her air of total efficiency, "I'll see if the Headmaster is available."

She disappeared through a door on the right and I sat down and waited patiently. The minutes ticked by until eventually she reappeared looking flustered again.

"I'm very sorry but I'm afraid the Headmaster is busy at the moment," she said. "I'll just see if there's a member of the English staff available to talk to you."

This time she disappeared through a door on the left and once again I waited. But not for long. She was back almost immediately.

"Unfortunately you've caught us in the middle of a lesson," she explained apologetically, "and they all seem to be teaching at the moment. Could you possibly come back in half-an-hour? There'll be a break then."

I was beginning to feel distinctly unwanted - a bit like a character in a Kafka novel searching endlessly for an interview with someone in a position of authority and being thwarted at every turn. It was also becoming a strain on my nerves, continually building myself up to the big moment and then being let down. Still it wasn't the secretary's fault and I had nothing to gain by giving her a hard time. Meekly, I agreed to come back later and left. Much to my relief, I didn't meet the caretaker on the way out. I would have hated to disappoint him.

I went over to the small coffee shop and dawdled over a cup of coffee and a magazine until it was time to come back. This time the secretary looked a good deal more composed and I assumed this was due to the presence of the old man who stood beside her. She smiled as

I came in and said to her companion:

"Here he is, Herr Doktor, the new English assistant."

He walked towards me and shook me warmly by the hand.

"Welcome to Austria, Mr. Moss," he said in heavily accented English. "I am Dr. Burger."

"Pleased to meet you, sir," I replied.

"Up until last year," he continued, "I was Head of the English Department but, as you can see, I am an old man now and I shall soon be retiring. I have handed over the reins to a younger man, Herr Mroz, who will be your supervisor, but unfortunately he is attending a meeting elsewhere today. I'm afraid you'll have to wait until Monday to find out the details of your work here. However, I am happy to show you round the school and answer any questions you might have."

I was tempted to ask if anybody really wanted an assistant at all but fortunately I had the sense to restrain myself. I'd already realised that teachers were highly respected in Austria, even lowly ones like me, and a long serving head of department who also possessed a doctorate, which was even more highly respected, was probably like a god in the school. I could see quite clearly that he was not a good man to upset on my first day. The fact remained, though, that I had problems that wouldn't wait until Monday. I couldn't afford to spend the weekend in a hotel, especially if Mike found a place and I ended up paying for a room on my own. I hit him with the six-million dollar question.

"Has the school arranged any accommodation for me?"

He looked slightly taken aback.

"Well no. It's never been our policy to provide accommodation for our assistants. We have no mechanism for arranging it. Where are you living at the moment?"

He was genuinely distressed when he heard I was living in a hotel and clearly understood the financial problem this was causing me, but officially the school had no formal responsibility for finding me somewhere to live.

"But, of course, we do have a responsibility for your general well-being all the same."

He scratched his head for a few moments considering the predicament.

"Well," he said at last, "there are two things I can think of. The first is to put you in touch with Bud Ryan in the English faculty at the university. He's an American who was once my English assistant here and decided to stay on. He has experience of finding accommodation for the American students who come and study in Innsbruck. The other thing we can do is talk to *Herr Professor* Reitenberger here at the school. I believe he has recently separated from his wife and is living back at his mother's house. He's planning to sell the flat soon but these things take time and he might like to have someone in there on a temporary basis, you know, to keep an eye on things."

That sounded much more like it. I rather fancied the idea of a flat to myself even if it was only a temporary measure.

"I think it's best if we go and find *Herr Professor* Reitenberger first," continued Dr. Burger. "You'll need to meet him anyway since he'll be one of your colleagues. I'm sure he'll be willing to help."

We found Hans Reitenberger in a classroom on the second floor, writing English vocabulary on the blackboard. He was an extremely impressive figure, cast in the classic ski instructor mould. Well over six feet tall, with a deep suntan even in October, he bore a striking resemblance to the French actor Jean-Paul Belmondo. As a student he had been an Austrian international slalom skier - the local equivalent of playing football for England. His English was excellent, spoken with a strong Australian accent. In fact, at first, I thought he was Australian, despite his eminently Austrian name, but as I slowly attuned to his accent, I picked up the underlying influence of his native German. I did have to listen for it, though, and I decided there and then to cultivate a touch of the Innsbruck accent in my German. It had the effect of an 'aural illusion', deceiving a native speaker far more effectively than good grammar and a wide vocabulary.

After the highly formal introductions, Dr. Burger explained my predicament to Hans. He was only too willing to help.

"By all means," he said. "Move in tomorrow if you want to. I don't like the flat being empty; my wife might try to repossess it."

"That's great," I said, much relieved. "Where is it?"

"Well, that's the only problem. The flat's not actually in town. Do you have a car?"

My heart sank again. I didn't have a car or, for that matter, a licence, and anyway I wanted to live in Innsbruck, preferably near the school. I wasn't very good at getting up in the morning.

"No, I don't drive at all in fact," I said. "How far away is it?"

"It's in Axams, one of the little villages up in the mountains. There's a regular bus service during the day, but they only run every two hours in the evening. You might feel a bit isolated."

I agreed but I could see that I might not have any choice, at least to begin with.

"Do you mind if I have a chat with Bud Ryan first?" I asked. "There's a chance he might know of somewhere more permanent and in town."

"Not at all. You ought to check out all your options, it's only sensible."

He took out a pen and scribbled something on a scrap of paper.

"Here's my home telephone number," he said, handing it to me. "If you're still not fixed up tonight, ring me and I'll drive you up there tomorrow."

I took the paper and thanked him profusely but I hoped desperately I wouldn't actually need it.

Chapter Four

Half-an-hour later, I was back where I'd been the previous day, seated outside on the piazza at Moby Dick's. As far as I could tell, Bud Ryan hadn't appeared yet and I guessed he was still teaching somewhere in the faculty building across the way. All in all, I wasn't much further forward than the last time I'd sat here and I was far from impressed by the legendary Teutonic gift for administration I'd heard so much about or the legendary Austrian hospitality, come to that. My overwhelming first impression of Innsbruck was that I was somehow just a burden to the people at the school and not really wanted.

I also missed desperately not having somewhere to call my own. It didn't need to be much as long as it was relatively permanent and I could unpack all my possessions. But it did need to be convenient; somewhere I could go back to whenever I felt like it. There was nothing more tiring or depressing than wandering around aimlessly just killing time. Bud Ryan had already told Dr. Burger on the phone that he didn't hold out much hope of finding me anywhere and Hans' flat, despite its superficial attraction wasn't really suitable. It was neither permanent nor convenient. Lessons began punctually at five to eight, as I'd already discovered that morning, which meant getting up very early to catch the bus into town if I had a class, and finished around lunchtime. I would therefore have to decide each day whether to go home or wander around all afternoon so as to be available to do something in the evening. I knew full well that once I'd gone back up into the mountains and got settled, I wouldn't want to come all the way back into town again. I knew this from experience having spent the previous year at college living six miles out of town with no car and an irregular bus service. My life had been governed by time-tables and I had missed out on a lot of college social activities by going home during the day and not coming back, or being forced to leave early to catch the last bus home. But at least there I'd had the use of the college common room during the day. Here in Innsbruck it would have to be coffee shops and park benches. It was a depressing thought.

"Hi," said a voice, interrupting my depressing thought. "Are you

Iain?"

I looked up and found a large man of about thirty with short-cropped hair towering over me.

"That's right," I said, standing up. "You must be Bud."

"Sure am. How ya doing?"

He held out an enormous fist and we shook hands.

"Let's go inside," he said. "It's too damn cold out here."

We found a table in the plastic interior and Bud ordered two large beers. The last thing I wanted after the previous night was more beer but I didn't like to refuse.

"So you're looking for a place to live?" he said, coming straight to the point.

I nodded.

"So is every new assistant in Innsbruck," he continued, "and probably all over Austria. It happens every year and has been ever since I first came here. I'm sick and tired of writing to the schools about it. They never take any notice. I spent my first six months in a hotel living out of suitcases. I wasn't the first and I sure as hell won't be the last."

He stopped for a moment and lit a cigarette, taking a large puff before going on.

"I presume that's what you're doing?"

"Yes, and I'm fed up with it already," I said. "What are my chances of finding somewhere quickly?"

"Virtually nil, unfortunately. We've had a high intake of students from Notre Dame University this year on exchange scholarships and they've snapped up just about everything that's going. I had a quick phone round this morning to try and find you somewhere but there's just nothing doing. I'm sorry."

It didn't come as much of a surprise.

"Oh well, it looks like I'm in for a stay in Axams after all," I said.

"What is there in Axams?"

I explained about Hans' flat. Bud let out a long low whistle.

"Gee, I know that place. It's beautiful and so's the village. I would have given my right arm for a place like that when I first came here. So would all the others still looking for places. What's your problem? Take it."

"Yes, I know. But it's so far out." I outlined the many problems I could foresee living in Axams but Bud was unconvinced.

He shrugged his shoulders.

"It beats the hell out of a hotel, that's all I can say. In fact, it beats the hell out of anything you could afford in town, even if you could find something. Temporary and inconvenient it may be, but it's a pretty damn good place to start. At least it's somewhere to hang your hat for a while."

I knew he was right of course. I had to be realistic.

"OK. I'm convinced. I'll ring Hans this afternoon and arrange to move in tomorrow. But if you do hear of anything in town that looks suitable, can you give me first option?"

"Yea. I'll do that."

He ordered another round of beers, even though I was barely halfway through my first one, and lit another cigarette.

"It may not seem like it at the moment, but you've really fallen on your feet with this posting you know."

"You're right. It doesn't seem like it at the moment."

He laughed.

"Ah, but it will though, it will. Come next July, you'll be looking back at this moment and wishing you were here starting all over again. That's what happened to me and I felt just as bad as you do now at the beginning. But, at the end, I couldn't bear to leave the place."

"So you didn't."

"Nope. I've been here ever since, and here I'll stay until they put me in my box."

I was curious how he'd managed to stay in Innsbruck so long. After all, if what he said was true, I might just want to use the same method myself one day.

"How did you fix it?" I asked.

He shrugged.

"It wasn't too hard really and I had some luck as well along the way. First of all, I stayed on a second year at the school as their assistant and started doing a teaching degree part time at the university. Doing that I got to know a lot of the people in the English faculty and when I finished the second year and was desperately looking around for another job, I got offered a two year post as a junior lecturer. I finished the degree and married an Austrian girl just in time to pick up a permanent job in the faculty when the contract finished. Everything just seemed to fall right, you see. But it was a gamble. I had to decide not to go back to the States to finish my Masters. If you like, that was my stake, and I won the jackpot."

"But what was so special about it? What made you take that big a risk in the first place?"

He took a slug of beer and a puff on his cigarette, gathering his thoughts.

"Well, it was a mixture of all sorts of things really, some of which were really important then but are actually irrelevant now. I mean to start with you're suddenly handed this amazing opportunity to take a year out of the real world with virtually no responsibilities and more freedom than you're ever likely to have in your life again. Even compared to university its unreal - no exams, no lectures, no essays. You get paid an exorbitant amount of money for doing very little and you have all the time in the world to make good use of it."

"I'm sure you're right," I said, "but you could just as well say that about any posting as an assistant."

"Maybe so, but Austria is still better than most. They pay a lot more than any other country except Switzerland and the work is a hell of a lot easier. For the first two weeks, you don't do anything except sit in the classroom and listen, just to get a feel of how they do things. After that you always work with a teacher in the class to make sure you don't pump the kids full of left-wing anti-catholic propaganda. In most countries, you're just left on your own with a class for an hour and that's damn hard work. Actually, you can have the best of both worlds here. If you don't like the work, you can just sit back and let the teacher run the class. If you enjoy it and you're competent, they'll let you run the whole lesson if you want to. And the teacher is always there to bail you out if you get into trouble. As for the town, you'd be hard pushed to find somewhere better to live for a year, now wouldn't you? It's big enough to find plenty to do and small enough to be friendly. And if you like skiing then this is paradise."

"That's why I applied for it. What about the school?"

"Well, in my far from humble opinion, it's the best school in Innsbruck. By Austrian standards it's fairly relaxed and easy going. The kids are fun, the staff, by and large, are young and friendly, it has social events outside of work. It's a good place."

I was desperate to find out something about Herr Mroz, my new supervisor. After all he had my fate in his hands for the next year. I asked Bud if he knew him.

"Everyone in Innsbruck knows Reiner Mroz," he replied, grinning broadly. "He's a local institution."

"That sounds ominous. I'm not sure I fancy working for a local institution."

"Oh, you'll like him. He's a real character - a total non-conformist. You don't get many of those in government jobs in Austria. He's outspoken, doesn't give a damn who he offends, drinks like a fish, and smokes sixty a day. And he's divorced, which is still frowned upon here, lives with one of my students from the university, which is also frowned upon, and still talks like a mountain yokel. He's quite a guy."

"I'm surprised he survives. I would have thought that the authorities would have tried to get rid of him."

"Ah, but he's good you see. Damn good. Year in year out his pupils get the best results in the area and that's more important to the parents than his personality. Everyone wants his kids to be taught English by Reiner. Not only that but he's clever too. When I was at the school, he was just an ordinary teacher. Now, at thirty-five, he's Head of Department, near as dammit, when old Burger finally goes, and Tyrolean delegate to the National Education Council. That's a very important post, carries a lot of weight. In ten years he'll either be a headmaster or something big in the Ministry of Education. He's done very well has Reiner."

"I suppose that makes him a real pain to work for?"

"Well, nobody knows, you see. This is his first year as acting Head of Department and you're his first assistant. He can be a hard bastard if he wants and my advice would be not to cause him any problems. If he thinks you're good for him, he'll look after you, but he's very young to have that job and he'll hammer you if he thinks you're screwing him up."

He took a last drag on his cigarette and stubbed it out.

"The authorities don't really like assistants, you see. They're an unknown quantity. For all they know, you might create havoc in their nice orderly system, preaching Marxism and screwing the pupils. If you settle in and do a nice, quiet, efficient job, they'll all breathe a sigh of relief and assume Reiner knows how to keep an assistant under control. If you don't, it'll reflect very badly on him, so you're quite important to Reiner in many ways."

I greeted this with mixed feelings. I had no outrageous religious or political views, so that wouldn't be a problem, and I had some experience of teaching English conversation so I thought I could handle that side of it alright. But I decided to keep very quiet about my escapades while teaching during the summer. Against all the rules I had gone out with one of my students and been caught by the two spinsters who ran the courses. It had been no great crime. The girl was almost the same age as me and it had just been a typical summer romance complicated by the fact that I was temporarily her teacher. But I had been banned from any future work with the organization. In that case, it had been of no real importance whatsoever, but here it was totally out of the question. According to the authorities in Vienna, it was actually against the law to conduct a relationship with a pupil and the absolute minimum penalty was being sent home in disgrace. I didn't think my university would be very impressed if it happened to me.

I noticed Bud's glass was empty and suggested we have another round but he declined.

"No thanks," he said, "I'm due home for lunch." Then, as an afterthought, "Hey, why don't you come and join us? There's always plenty."

Being English, I assumed he was just being polite, so I said I was meeting someone. It was a long while before I learned that in Austria an invitation to eat was only offered if it was sincerely meant and I turned down a lot of free meals in my first few months in Innsbruck. Anyway the lunchtime beer and the disturbed night's sleep were taking their toll and I planned to go back to the hotel and rest for a while before meeting Mike.

We left the restaurant and I said goodbye to Bud.

"Don't forget to phone Hans," he said, as he prepared to leave. "I'm sure you'll be just fine up in Axams and if I hear of anything in the meantime, I'll let you know."

"Thanks Bud. And thanks for the chat. I feel better already."

"Don't worry. You'll love it here. You'll always regret it if you don't make the most of it. Anyway I'll see you again soon. I often go out with the people from the school. I'll take a rain check then."

He waved goodbye and I wandered back to the hotel.

When I got to the Consulate at four, I met Mike coming out. Even from a distance I could see the big grin on his face. As I approached, he shouted jubilantly:

"I think I've found somewhere to live."

He waited for me to reach him and then said excitedly:

"I think I've got a place. The secretary upstairs knows a woman with a room to let. She's taking me to see it when she finishes work at five-thirty."

I cursed my bad luck. I'd toyed with the idea of coming over earlier since I'd had the whole afternoon free but I'd decided to wait. Mike had now benefited from being there first.

"I don't suppose she's got two rooms by any chance?" I asked without any real hope.

"No, it's just the one," said Mike. "Anyway, you know as well as I do it wouldn't be a good idea to live in the same place. We'd never speak any German."

He was right of course. We wanted to live within easy reach of each other but not in the same house.

"I take it that means you aren't fixed up yet?" he continued.

I briefly filled him in on the morning's events. He understood my reservations about the flat but was able to offer one glimmer of hope.

"How long can you stay in Axams?"

"I'm not sure. A month or so I think. There's no big hurry as far as I know."

"Well that might just work out then. I was given a few numbers to ring this morning at school and I tried them all. Most of them were useless but there was one guy with a room to let from the beginning of November. I said I'd let him know just in case I couldn't get anything else but it might be just what you're looking for. We could go and see it tomorrow."

"Why not? I've got nothing to lose. Can you ring him and arrange it?"

"Ok, but I want to keep my options open for a while just in case I don't get fixed up tonight. I mean, at a pinch, I could beg someone at the school to put me up for a month and then move in there. Is that all right?"

"That's fair enough. You found it."

"But if I'm on to a winner tonight I'll arrange for us to see the other one tomorrow."

"Ok, that's great, thanks."

At least going to Axams wouldn't be quite so bad if I knew I had somewhere permanent to move into at the end of the month.

"I suppose I'd better go and see the Consul then," I said.

"It doesn't take long. You just fill in a form so they know who you are and who to contact if you break your neck skiing. Then the Assistant Consul gives you a two minute pep talk and tells you to be a good boy and fly the flag and then it's all over."

"Sounds like a waste of time."

"Well you never know. We might need help one day. It's worth five minutes."

As Mike had predicted, I was in and out in five minutes, not greatly enlightened by the Assistant Consul's pep talk. He was young and inexperienced and obviously hadn't been there very long. He didn't seem to know much about Innsbruck or about living abroad and I sympathized with him. It was a strain for both of us and I think the relief was mutual when it was over. I found Mike in the coffee house across the road up to his elbows in a large cake consisting of cream and catering custard sandwiched between three slabs of flaky pastry and topped with sticky pink icing. He looked up rather guiltily as I entered and then defiantly continued eating.

"That'll spoil your appetite for dinner," I said, sitting down.

"Dinner's not for ages yet," he replied between mouthfuls, "and anyway I didn't get any lunch."

"I don't think I'll risk it. I'll stick to coffee."

I attracted the attention of the waitress and placed my order and then turned back to Mike.

"Come on then. How did you get on at your school?"

Carefully he finished the last mouthful of cake, pushed away his plate, dabbed his mouth gently with a napkin and then, with a theatrical flourish, produced a piece of paper from his jacket pocket with all the élan of a conjurer drawing a rabbit from a hat.

"Voilà. My timetable. The elusive Herr Gell finally turned up."

"That's great," I said with a slightly forced smile. "What's he like?"

"He's alright. About forty, you know, very friendly and he's put a lot of work into my timetable. It's very reasonable. I've got every Friday and Saturday free which is a big help. I'm working twelve lessons at his school and four at the other one. The only problem is that all of those are in the afternoon because technical colleges work different hours from the ordinary grammar schools but you can't have everything."

"It sounds like he's really pulled out all the stops for you," I said enviously. "I hope Reiner Mroz is as generous to me."

"I'm sure he will be. After all it's no skin off their nose, is it? It just means putting a bit of thought into it."

"I suppose so. What about your school? What's that like?"

"It's what they call an *Akademisches Akadamie*. It's for the brighter more academic pupils, a bit like a grammar school I suppose. They concentrate on the arts and the classics and that sort of thing. I must admit it's a very formal kind of place, though I haven't seen much of the kids yet. And the technical college is the complete opposite. Older kids without much academic ability studying mainly vocational stuff. I mean one of my classes is full of budding travel agents."

"Just like the rest of the town."

"But that's just it, you see. They're training them for the job market and the biggest growth industry in Austria is travel. It seems like a good system to me. What about your school?"

"Somewhere in the middle I guess. More like a secondary school but with an emphasis on science and technology. It's got chemistry and physics labs, a computer room and a machine shop and it's quite new and modern.

"I saw it, remember?"

"Of course you did. Yesterday was such a long time ago I'd forgotten. Anyway according to Bud it's much more relaxed and easy going than most schools."

"Well that's an advantage. You'll probably find it easier to get to know people. Especially as all your work is in the one school."

I shrugged.

"I guess its swings and roundabouts. You'll get to meet more people working two schools so it'll all balance out in the end."

"You're probably right. Anyway I'm taking the first step on Sunday. I've been invited to dinner with Gell and his family and some of the English staff from the school. It's a good chance to meet them informally before I start work for real."

I was quite glad in a way when five-thirty came and Mike went off to meet the receptionist. I'd started to feel the first hint of jealousy and resentment as we talked and I didn't want it to show. Of course I was pleased for him that things were starting to sort themselves out, but it was galling that everything was working out so much quicker for him than for me. It also struck me as an ironic twist of fate that I'd ended up living in an isolated mountain village when Mike was the one who spoke German well enough to be able to cope with it. It didn't occur to me at the time that this was precisely why I was the one who could benefit most from the experience.

I was back on my own again with time to kill until Mike had finished his business. If I'd had any money, I would have wandered around the shops till they closed. I found spending money on things I wanted but didn't need highly therapeutic when I was down and the array of goods in Innsbruck was extremely attractive. There was one place in particular, a large department store in the middle of the high street that I really liked. It was beautifully laid out, tastefully lit and warm and inviting. Its chief attraction of course was the simple fact that I had no money and the very unavailability of the items on display was enticing. But it was ultimately frustrating and I decided to use the time sensibly and go and phone Hans instead.

I had no idea how to make a phone call in Austria. I didn't even know what coins were needed. However, according to the information on the back of my tourist map, there was a main post office in one of the side roads just up from the big stone archway at the top of the main street. It was open till midnight every day and had metered telephone facilities. I'd come across those before. Instead of putting money in a coin box, the phone had a built-in timing device linked to central register which clocked the cost of a call anywhere in the world. You could then simply pay over the counter. Under the circumstances, this seemed like the best way of doing things.

When I arrived at the post office, there was some kind of fracas taking place and I could hear the dulcet tones of an Australian shouting:

"I'm not paying that much. That bastard is trying to cheat me."

Inside I found two policemen attempting to restrain a very irate Australian. One of the policemen wore a badge bearing the legend 'English Specialist' and he was explaining in excellent English that it wasn't possible that there had been a mistake and that the gentleman would have to pay what he owed and then they could all forget the incident. It was obvious that he was wasting his breath, though, and that the Australian wasn't going to listen to reason and he was soon dragged off out of the building defiantly shouting and swearing.

That was a great start for me. Here I was an English speaker, looking for assistance, and the last one in had just had his own one man riot. I wasn't expecting a very warm reception but the clerk at the desk seemed unperturbed by the incident.

"Another satisfied customer," he said laconically.

I summoned up my best German and explained what I wanted to do.

"That's fine," he said. "It's a bit unusual to make a local call that way and it'll cost you a little bit more but it's not a problem."

He fiddled with a register under the counter and then directed me to booth number three.

My call didn't take very long. Hans was out but he'd left a message with his mother that if I phoned and wanted the flat she should tell me that he'd meet me at the hotel at two o'clock the next afternoon. She had some difficulty getting the message across, repeating it three times, more slowly each time, until I finally got it, but we made it eventually. The combination of the telephone and her broad Tyrolean accent was lethal. I went back to the counter and paid for the call and a pamphlet on international dialling caught my eye. I picked it up and flicked through it, just for future reference really, but I was surprised at how easy it was and how cheap. Provided you knew the local STD code you could dial straight through to anywhere in England. I thought about it for a few minutes and then made a decision. I was going to ring home.

At university, I'd always called home regularly every Friday night and, far from being a chore, it had always been something I looked forward to. With my father, I talked about my work and general college activities and my mother normally lent a sympathetic ear to girlfriend troubles and the like. They provided a useful intellectual and emotional sounding board for me and, in return, they enjoyed sharing my experience of life at university, something neither of them had ever had any contact with before. It was Friday night and I didn't see why the fact that I was almost a thousand miles away should make any difference.

Making the call was childishly simple and I had a ringing tone almost as soon as I had stopped dialling the number. I hung on there with bated breath, waiting for someone to answer, hoping desperately that they were at home. After what seemed like an eternity, the phone was picked up and I heard my mother reel off the number. At first I was just too choked to say anything and she repeated the number several times before I managed to force out the words:

"Hello, it's me."

"Hello, dear," she said. "I thought you might ring tonight."

Conversation was a bit stilted at first. We were all a little emotional and none of us could think of anything sensible to say. But things quickly relaxed and I began to pour out everything that had happened since I left home. Soon we were all gabbling away like mad with my parents pulling the phone in and out of each other's hands in their eagerness to talk. I'd originally intended to restrict myself to just two minutes but I got totally carried away. However, once we hit the six minute mark, I knew I had to stop or join the Australian in the local police station when I couldn't pay the bill.

"I'm going to have to go," I said reluctantly, "or I won't have enough money to pay. I'll ring you again soon."

"Well you take care," said my mother, "and make sure you eat properly and dress up warm and if you need any money ring and......"

"I will mum, I will, I promise."

That was a lie. It had already cost them more than they could afford to get me there. I'd starve before I asked them for more money. Reluctantly I said goodbye and put down the phone.

I walked back out into the cold, dark street and headed towards the bright lights of Maria-Theresien-Strasse. But I wasn't really there any more. I was somewhere far far away in a little town in England.

Chapter Five

"Sorry about last night," I said to Mike over breakfast the next morning, "I didn't mean to ruin the evening."

I'd rather spoiled Mike's evening after my phone call home. He'd come back happy and excited about the room he'd found and I just hadn't been able to work up any enthusiasm. I'd sunk into a bout of homesickness and depression and he'd given up trying to snap me out of it in the end. It had not been much fun for either of us.

"Oh, that's alright. I sympathise. Anyway I should have been a bit more sensitive instead of coming back crowing about how well I'd done. Still it'll be your turn this morning with any luck."

Mike had rung Herr Orzsky, who was offering the room at the end of the month and arranged for us to see it at ten o'clock.

"How much are you paying?" I asked. I had no idea at all what a room was likely to cost.

"The landlady's asking 1100 schillings a month. That includes heating and lighting, use of the kitchen and bathroom and a woman who comes in to clean all the rooms once a week. Did I tell you she's married to the chief of police?"

"Who? The cleaner?"

He looked at me coolly over the top of his glasses.

"The landlady, idiot. Gell said that I should expect to pay between a thousand and fifteen hundred schillings a month so I think it's a fair rent."

Eleven hundred schillings was about £36 which didn't seem unreasonable.

"And you say you've got the whole of the top floor?"

"You really weren't with it last night, were you? She lets the whole of the top floor. There are three bedsits and a separate kitchen and bathroom."

"Well that's good. It means you'll get to know some people."

"That's what I'm hoping for."

"Just as long as nobody English moves in."

"I thought about that. It would be a real drag. But I think she said one was Austrian and the other was a Belgian so that shouldn't be a problem."

After a leisurely breakfast, we checked out of the hotel. The old lady was very kind and agreed to look after our luggage until lunchtime, saving us the trouble of going and dumping it at the station. We then wandered up to the high street to take a tram from the main terminus in the town centre.

There were only two tram services around the town itself; the Number One and the Number Six. The rest ran between the outskirts of Innsbruck and the nearer villages such as Igls and Mutters. Buses served the rest of the town and the ubiquitous single decker 'Post' buses ran out and up into the more isolated mountain villages. Mike's house was at the far end of the Number One's route, out to the east, and the Number Six ran first east then north towards the foot of the Hafelekar Mountain in the Nordkette chain. We needed the number six since the place I was going to see was almost at the foot of the mountain itself.

Trams were an expensive way of travelling around Innsbruck. A single ticket cost ten schillings and was valid for one journey including a change to the other tram route. This meant that although a long cross-town journey justified a tram ride, short trips were a waste of money. You could cut the cost to eight schillings by buying books of ten tickets and fortunately Herr Gell had explained this to Mike. When the tram arrived, we bought a book each from the conductor sitting in his little wooden box at the back and went and sat down on a hard wooden seat.

For much of the journey, we followed the route I had taken to my school the day before. But once we reached the large railway viaduct, the tram turned northwards and proceeded down a small narrow road with houses on one side and little shops, set into the grubby arches of the viaduct, on the other. Presently, this broadened out into a much prettier tree-lined avenue, bordered by a park and separated from the viaduct by a row of elegant houses. Mike began to look around him and then back to his map a few times and then said:

"Ours is the next stop, I think."

The tram rumbled to a halt a few moments later at the top of the avenue, the centre doors shushed open and we jumped off. The house lay around the corner in the next street - another wide avenue, surrounded by terraced houses and boasting a long grass covered island in the middle planted with trees and shrubs.

"Hey," I said to Mike, "this is rather nice."

"Very picturesque," he agreed.

We found the house without difficulty but deciding which bell to press was rather more of a problem. We'd come to see Herbie Orzsky but all three bells were marked 'H. Orzsky' with a little epithet in brackets indicating their position in the family hierarchy; junior, middle or senior.

"That's a good start," said Mike. "Which one do we press?"

"Why not start at the bottom and work up?" I suggested.

"Alright then. Here goes."

He pressed the bell marked 'H. Orzsky - Middle' and we waited. Nothing happened. He pressed it a second time and a few moments later the intercom beside the door crackled and a sleepy voice said:

"Who is it?"

"My name's Mike Jensen," announced Mike. "I rang yesterday about a room to let. Are you Herbie?"

"That's me," said the voice. "Just hang on."

There was a short silence followed by a sharp buzz as the lock was released remotely and we pushed our way through the heavy iron door. Inside there were two flights of steps, one going down, presumably to the cellar, and the other going up to a doorway on the landing and then continuing on to the other floors. The intervening space was strewn with several bicycles, a dustbin and two crates of empty wine bottles.

"Which way?" said Mike. "Up or down?"

As he spoke the door on the landing opened and a young man appeared wearing a knee-length dressing gown.

"Hi," he said, "I'm Herbie."

Mike adopted his, by now, habitual role as my interpreter.

"I'm Mike. I'm the one who rang you. This is Iain. He's the one who's actually interested in the room."

We all shook hands and Herbie showed us into the flat. Herbie was a good deal younger than I'd expected. He was about twenty-six with long hair and a droopy Mexican-style moustache. In fact, he looked more like a student and I found it difficult to believe he owned the flat. I guessed that 'H. Orzsky - Senior' on the top floor must be his father. But this wasn't the case.

"Just to fill you in on the details," explained Herbie, "this whole building belongs to my parents who live in Vienna. My elder brother Hartmut and his wife, Irmi, have got the top floor and my little brother Hans has got the middle. I say little, he's twenty-three actually, but he's the youngest. We're a medical family. Papa's a consultant heart surgeon, Hartmut's a gynaecologist and Hans and me are medical students." He smiled broadly. "As a family we lack a certain amount of imagination. While we're studying, we have to let out the other rooms and manage the flat. Once we qualify, we can do what we like with them. Papa didn't want us to have any incentive to remain students too long."

"How much is the room?" asked Mike getting straight down to business.

"Well, I'd rather you saw the room first and decided whether you like it. There's no point in discussing all that if you hate the place. Come on it's over here."

He led us off to the right to a group of three doors each bearing the name of its occupier. He stopped in front of the middle one.

"There's a French girl here at the moment but she normally spends the weekend with her boyfriend." He knocked and waited a few moments but there was no sound from inside. Cautiously he opened the door and peered round before motioning to us to follow.

The room was enormous, the largest bedsitter I'd ever seen, and I knew at once that I was going to take it if the price was right. In one far flung corner, there was a bed and a cabinet, in the middle stood a low table flanked by two armchairs and, tucked into the enormous bay of the double windows, looking out onto the street, was a shabby but serviceable two-seater settee. It was big enough to give the illusion of separate living and sleeping areas if arranged properly. Dotted around the room was an ample complement of cupboards and drawers and, of course, a wardrobe. But what really caught my eye was a beautiful, tall, green object in the other corner, stretching from floor to ceiling, dominating the room.

"What on earth is that?" I asked Herbie.

"It's a stove. What we call a *Kacheloffen.* It's hard to heat a large room like this with an ordinary fire. But if you build a coal or log fire in there it radiates the heat all round the room."

"Presumably that costs quite a bit though?" said the ever practical Mike.

"Well obviously it's something you have to budget for in the cost of the room," replied Herbie. "But it's not exorbitant. A large bag of brick coal costs about two hundred schillings and that should last the whole winter. You only really need the coal as a base. There's a cellar full of logs downstairs."

"And how much is the rent?" I asked.

"Do you like it?" countered Herbie.

"Very much."

"In that case let's go and talk about it over a cup of coffee."

Providing a rapid conducted tour of the shared kitchen and bathroom en route Herbie led us through to a glass partitioned room at the other end of the flat.

"This is my sitting room," he said proudly. "My one advantage as a landlord though, in fact, everyone uses it when they want to, especially the record player." He smiled apologetically. "As you can see, I like the lived-in look.

Lived-in was a euphemism. It was a tip. There were books and records everywhere jostling for space with dirty cups and glasses. Its main function seemed to be to serve as a drinks' cellar, for almost every available inch of floor space was covered by a crate or a bottle. I rather liked it.

While we tried to find somewhere to sit, he went into the kitchen next door and came back carrying a small percolator and a bottle of milk. With difficulty, he managed to find three clean cups and filled them with coffee. Only once we were all comfortably seated with our drinks did he finally discuss money.

"Right, to business. The rent is nine hundred schillings per month of which I don't see a penny unfortunately. I simply give you a pile of bank transfers and you pay it each month direct into my parents' account. We don't have any gas, only electricity, and we split the quarterly bills between us. There is a telephone but it's incoming only and my parents pay the rental. Realistically, including the coal and your share of the electricity bill, the rent's going to average out at between a thousand and eleven hundred schillings a month. How's that sound?"

"It sounds good," I said. "How about the other people here?"

"At the moment there are four of us or five if you count the baby. There's Michelle, who's leaving of course, and in the room on the right of her there's Rolf and Inge and their baby Julia. She's only a year old but she's very good. The other room's empty at the moment but a friend called Eva is moving in at the end of November. She's a medical student and so's Rolf. You'd be the odd one out. It's always been a very happy flat and we usually have a lot of fun." He looked serious for a moment. "Actually we might have too much fun. I mean, we tend to make a lot of noise and you know, drink a bit. Well a lot actually. It's part of the syllabus at medical school. If you were planning to do much studying or anything you might find it a pain."

"I'm not planning on doing any studying actually." I said. "In fact, I'm planning on having fun and drinking a lot so you needn't worry."

His face brightened again.

"Oh good. One thing you will get to learn is lots of German. We can hardly put a sentence together in English."

In every way, the place seemed ideal. It was large and pleasant, it was in town near my school and I would be totally immersed in a German-speaking environment. The medical students were a bonus. There was no point in delaying the decision any longer.

"Well I like the place, Herbie. Can I take it?"

He smiled warmly.

"Of course. That's great. We'd be pleased to have you. You do know that you can't move in until November, though, don't you?"

"Yes, but that's not a problem. I've got somewhere temporary fixed up until then. Do you need a deposit or something?"

"No, that's OK. I trust you. You'll have to pay a month's rent in advance when you move in, though, if you can manage it."

"I don't think it will be a problem. I'm sure the school would help, even if I couldn't, anyway."

He held out his hand.

"Right it's a deal then."

We shook hands and Herbie let out a sigh of relief.

"Thank God that's over. I hate doing the landlord bit."

We all relaxed a bit after that and Herbie the landlord soon reverted to Herbie the student. Since Mike and I were both students too, we found we had a lot in common and we chatted away quite happily for half-an-hour or so until I glimpsed Mike out of the corner of my eye, surreptitiously glancing at his watch.

"Do you need to get back, Mike?" I asked.

"If you don't mind," he replied. "I promised to be at my place by twelve to meet the landlady's husband before he goes on duty. I'd hate to be late."

"That's no problem," said Herbie, "because I'm playing basketball soon. I don't think there's much else to discuss about the room. Why don't you give me a ring sometime nearer the date and we can sort out the details?"

"Sure, I'll do that," I said.

"OK then. I'll look forward to seeing you when you move in."

Back at the hotel I gave Mike a hand shifting his luggage.

"Sorry to rush off and leave you," he said, "but I don't want to make a bad impression by being late. Anyway I'd like to get there and get settled in, you know how it is."

"That's alright. I understand. You've done plenty for me already as it is."

"Well at least you've got your room sorted out. I think it'll work out well. It's a nice place."

"It's great. I just wish I could move in today."

"A month's not long and at least it's better than a hotel."

"Yes, of course."

He fished in his pocket for a piece of paper.

"This is my new telephone number," he said. "Why don't you give me a ring tomorrow and we can arrange to meet for lunch on Monday and compare notes?"

"Sure. We could go to one of those student refectories."

"That was what I was thinking."

We carried his bags over to the tram stop and waited for the Number One to appear. As it trundled into view I suddenly panicked at the idea of being left on my own.

"Listen Mike," I said. "You've got loads of luggage, why don't I come over with you and give you a hand? I've got several hours to kill before Hans comes."

"No. Don't be silly. I don't want to drag you all the way over there for nothing. I'll be fine once it's all loaded on the tram. It stops right outside the door."

I didn't press the point. He probably wanted to get settled in on his own.

"Ok, then, if you're sure. I'll give you a ring tomorrow. Good luck."

"And you. I hope it all works out in Axams."

"I'm sure it will."

I helped him onto the tram and watched it disappear shakily up the main street.

Chapter Six

I don't recall much about the next few hours. I remember wandering off to a small park by the river that I'd found the previous morning while walking and I remember coming back to the hotel to find Hans ready and waiting, but what happened in between has synthesized into one long feeling of misery and loneliness. After the initial feeling of elation at finding a suitable room at last, I'd come back to earth with a bump and the prospect of spending a month alone in a remote mountain village was frightening. Up until now I'd rather clung to Mike for support. I knew that I wouldn't have found the room without him and while acting as my interpreter he'd also done a good deal of my thinking for me. Now I was being thrown back on my own resources and, rather foolishly maybe, I felt pitifully inadequate.

"Hi, Iain," said Hans, as I walked into the hotel reception. "How goes it?"

"Fine thanks. Have you been waiting long?"

"No. I've just this minute got here. Are you all packed and ready?"

"Yes. My luggage is behind reception. I'll just get it."

I thanked the old lady for keeping an eye on my things and we carried them out to the car and loaded them into the boot.

"I'll take you the long way round," said Hans, as he moved off and threaded his way slowly through the streets of the Old Town. "It'll give you a chance to see something of Innsbruck."

I wasn't really in the mood for a guided tour but I certainly didn't want to hurt his feelings so we drove around the town for a while with Hans enthusiastically pointing out the places of interest. Like most of the population, he was very proud of Innsbruck but at that particular moment it was all rather lost on me. I just sat there sunk in a welter of self-pity, nodding now and again so as not to offend him. It was only once we left Innsbruck and began to climb up towards the mountains that I began to take more interest in my surroundings. The road out to Axams was a long, winding hill surrounded on both sides by woods full of tall pine trees and I was far more taken by the natural beauty than I had been by the man-made splendour of the palaces and churches down below. The sun flashing among the cool green of the trees and the cold grandeur of the distant mountains, drawing nearer with each curve in the road, began to lift my flagging spirits and a sense of curiosity and excitement started to vie with the depression and self-pity until the pendulum slowly swung back again. It felt like I'd spent the last week like that, swinging backwards and forwards between gloom and elation. Out of the woods the landscape was a rural patchwork of fields, dotted here and there with a cluster of houses and the occasional small church. The fields sloped gently away from the road with rocky outcrops very much in evidence around the periphery and rising high in the distance.

"We're nearly there," said Hans after a while. "We're on the outskirts now. You can see it's a farming community, mainly very small holdings worked by the whole family. They're Catholics of course and the community life tends to revolve around the church."

As we wound our way up through the narrow streets of the village, I saw the houses with a few cows grazing on a piece of land at the back and chickens pecking around in the yard at the front. Apart from that there didn't seem to be much else beside a church and an inn.

"There's a few shops further down on the other side of the village," said Hans again, as if reading my thoughts, "and a community centre but it's quite a small place really."

Hans' flat was just outside the village itself, standing among a group of similar new buildings on the hillside. These were in marked contrast to the old houses in the centre and appeared elite and aloof, as if looking down on the commoners in the valley.

"Most of the new houses were built because of the skiing on the *Axamer Lizum*, especially when it became an Olympic slope," he explained. "Quite a few of them are empty at this time of the year. They're owned by wealthier people in Innsbruck who let them out during the season and use them as weekend retreats the rest of the year. That was one of the things my wife hated about the place."

"How far's the *Lizum*?"

"A short drive. Far enough not to have spoiled the village but within easy reach for a full day on the slopes. It's ideal really. I was born here and I used the money I made as a ski-instructor in Australia, plus some money I won in professional competitions, to build myself a house. Then I divided it into two flats and sold one of them to pay off the loan. There's a young couple, the Müllers, in the other one."

A few moments later we drew up outside one of the houses and then parked the car in a basement level garage. Bud had certainly not been exaggerating when he'd said it was a beautiful place. Hans led me through a side door and up a staircase to a landing. On either side of the landing were two front doors labelled 'Flat A' and 'Flat B' and another staircase continued on up.

"This one's mine," said Hans indicating 'Flat A' on the right, "and that," he pointed to the other door," is where the Müllers live. I rang them this morning to let them know you were moving in. If you need anything I'm sure they'll be willing to help."

Inside the flat was bright and spacious, decorated and furnished with obvious care. I found it rather sad. He and his wife had clearly put a lot of effort into making it a home that would serve them for a good many years but it didn't seem to have been lived in very long. The furniture looked brand new and it seemed a terrible pity that the whole place was now going to be sold. I was curious about what had happened but I certainly had no intention of broaching the subject with Hans. There were seven rooms in all and I was to have the use of four of them - the kitchen and lounge on the left of the hallway and the bathroom and dining-room on the right.

"I'll leave the other three rooms locked if you don't mind," Hans explained. "It's not that I don't trust you, it's my wife I'm worried about. She's still got a key to the flat but I put new locks on these doors. They're piled high with all my stuff and she's still very bitter about the divorce. There's no telling what she might do. Some of the skiing equipment is quite valuable and there are all my cups and medals which are irreplaceable. I'd take them home but there's not a lot of room in my mother's flat."

"That's fine. Four rooms are more than enough for me anyway. What about your wife though? Is she likely to come here at all while I'm here?"

"Highly unlikely. There's no reason for her to. Everything's settled now save for the selling of the flat." He smiled mockingly.

"Anyway she's only a simple country girl and she's even less likely to come now there's a strange foreign man in the flat. I mean you might rape her or something."

My only other concern was that there didn't seem to be anywhere for me to sleep. I wondered whether the armchair in the lounge was really a sofa-bed or something.

"Oh sorry," said Hans when I asked him. "I forgot to tell you about the bedroom upstairs. It used to be my study but I turned it into a bedroom when the marriage started to go wrong. I think you'll be alright up there. Come on I'll show you."

We left the flat and he led me up the other flight of stairs leading off the landing. At the top, there was another small landing with just one door directly ahead. He fiddled with the keys on his keyring, found the right one and opened it up.

"Your stuff will be perfectly safe up here whatever happens," he said as we went in. "She hasn't got a key to this lock either."

It was a pleasant room, similar to a study at university, equipped with a large double bed and a desk placed in front of the window so as to pick up the panoramic view of the mountains. For a room that hadn't been used for a while it looked amazingly clean and dust-free and the sheets and duvet cover looked freshly laundered.

"My mother insisted I drive her up here this morning to get the place ready for you," Hans explained. "She wouldn't have a stranger believing the Austrians didn't know how to treat a guest."

I was touched by this, especially as I hardly classed as an invited guest.

"Please thank her for me and tell her I have the very highest opinion of Austrian hospitality."

"She'll like that. Hospitality is very important here in Austria. Right, well I think that's it. You've seen all there is. We'd better get your bags out of the car and get you settled in."

Hans hovered around for a while but there wasn't really much more he could do. He took me next door to say hello to the Müllers but they were out and drew me a little map of the village so I'd know where to catch the bus on Monday but beyond that he'd already done as much as he could, which was more than enough in any case. He seemed to feel, though, that there was something more he ought to be doing for me to help me settle in but it was really down to me now. In fact, I was quite happy to be left alone. I'd recovered from my earlier panic and was looking forward to a little solitude. I wanted to get my things unpacked and have a good look round the flat, something I felt inhibited about doing while Hans was still there. Eventually, after asking me for the hundredth time if there was anything else he could do and checking yet again that I had his telephone number at home, he reluctantly prepared to leave. He gave me the keys and said:

"There's not much food or anything like that in the place but if you do find anything you want just take it. I think there's still some booze in the lounge and feel free to use the stereo and the colour television. You know, just make yourself at home. There's a restaurant just up the road and you can get a good dinner there quite cheaply. I've marked it on your map."

He went to the door and then stopped again.

"By the way, do you need any money?"

"No, but thanks very much. I'm alright for the moment."

"Ok then. Well goodbye. Take care."

Before I had time to do anything he was back again.

"Oh and while I remember, don't worry about rent. You can pay me something towards the lighting and the heating when you get paid."

I thanked him again and he disappeared, though not with any great air of conviction. I waited patiently for a few moments until I heard him coming back again.

"If you have any problems you can let me know at school on Monday. In fact, I'll probably call in again tomorrow just to make sure you're OK."

"Hans, I'm really alright honestly. I'm used to living on my own. I've been doing it for years. Now go off and do whatever you normally do on a Saturday afternoon. I don't want to take up your whole weekend."

"Well if you're quite sure..."

"I'm sure. Honestly."

He left again but this time I heard the door close downstairs and the sound of a car starting. I looked out of the window and eventually saw him driving back down towards the village still unconvinced I'm certain that I would survive more than five minutes on my own.

I felt a glorious sense of freedom when he'd gone. Temporary or not, I had my own flat for the next few weeks and I was going to make the most of it. Paradoxically, after my earlier reluctance to leave Mike, I was glad to be on my own again. It was the first real privacy I had had for over a week after sharing rooms in the hostel in Vienna and in the hotel with Mike. I set about exploring the flat with enthusiasm, wandering round all the rooms at my disposal looking at everything, sitting on all the chairs and opening all the cupboards like a child. I had everything I needed in the way of amenities; cooker, fridge-freezer, stereo, colour television and enough alcohol in the lounge to keep me permanently legless for the next month. Even the larder yielded some basic necessities such as tea and coffee although there was nothing substantial in the way of food. It was too late to buy anything now as well. Most shops closed at lunchtime on a Saturday, even in Innsbruck, and I had to resign myself to two main meals over the weekend in restaurants. On Monday, I would have to sort myself out and do some shopping. I couldn't afford to live on restaurant food.

When I'd finished exploring, I carried my bags up to my room to unpack. My luggage reflected my priorities in life; a tape recorder and three boxes of cassettes, a guitar, as many books as I could carry and whatever clothes would fit into the remaining space. My mother and I had argued for days over what I should take, particularly over the lack of sensible clothing, but I'd won in the end by promising to buy more clothes once I knew what sort of things I'd need. I'd tried to explain that the cassettes and books were like old friends and that they were the things which would keep me sane if things got really bad but, like most mothers, she believed firmly that the key to mental health was warm underwear and washing behind your ears. As for the guitar, it served mainly as a monument to years of lack of practice, progress and ability but there is something extraordinarily comforting nonetheless about strumming away arrhythmically while singing out of key – unless you happen to live in the room next door. With great care, I laid out my possessions, arranging the books alphabetically on the bookshelves and then, as an afterthought, threw all the clothes into a drawer.

A few hours later I was beginning to regret my cavalier attitude to my clothing and almost wishing I'd listened to my mother. It was bitterly cold outside the flat, much colder than it had been down the valley in Innsbruck, and I was shivering after a few steps in the night air. It was also unnervingly quiet, the silence broken only by the occasional noise from one of the smallholdings in the distance. The air was heavy with farmyard smells. Only a few of the houses round about were lit and distant lights glittered here and there up in the now invisible mountains, seemingly suspended in mid-air. I could see the restaurant Hans had recommended a few hundred yards up the road. It looked like a new place and I assumed it had been built, like the houses around it, to cash in on the ski trade during the winter. It probably also provided a Saturday night out or a place to celebrate a special occasion for the people in the neighbouring villages. I would have preferred something more ethnic by choice like the old hotel in town but it was too cold to go wandering around the village looking for a restaurant and, anyway, I would have stuck out like a sore thumb in a local inn. It was out of season and nobody would expect to find a stranger, let alone a foreigner, up here at this time of the year. I'd be far less conspicuous in the tourist trap.

The restaurant was virtually deserted and I chose a table tucked away in a corner by the window. I liked eating out, but I always felt self-conscious eating alone or, worse still sharing a table with strangers, and I was glad it wasn't busy. I also noticed with some relief from a small slip of paper on the table that Saturday night Tyrolean evenings didn't start until December. I wasn't quite up to thigh slapping locals in Lederhosen accompanied by oompah bands just yet. I think you needed to acclimatise first.

I'd done an excellent job of hiding myself away and it was some time before the waitress noticed me sitting there. Hurriedly, she grabbed a menu and came rushing over to the table.

"*Grüss Gott, Mein Herr.* Sorry to keep you waiting. I didn't see you come in. Would you like something to drink?"

"Yes thank you. I'll have a large beer please."

I could tell from the flicker of surprise in her eyes that she'd picked up I was foreign immediately. Mind you, she didn't need to be Professor Higgins. With my command of German, it only needed one sentence. But she was too polite to comment on the fact and merely said, "Very good, *Mein Herr*" and left me to read the menu.

There's always a brief thrill of anticipation when you open up the menu in a restaurant, wondering what gastronomic delights you'll find inside, but my thrill turned to one of horror when I saw the prices. It looked alarmingly expensive, especially compared to *Der Goldene Löwe*, although in retrospect it was about average for the area. I discounted half the menu immediately on the grounds of price and resigned myself to a bowl of soup and a side salad. However, after a thorough inspection I found something called *Bauernplatte* - farmer's dish - which was just about in my price range. I didn't know what it was but I ordered it anyway when the waitress came back with my beer and pulled my book out of my pocket to while away the time until it was ready.

It was a big disappointment when it came. I'd been half expecting some kind of stew or meat with sauerkraut but what I got was a wooden board covered with slices of various sausages and cheeses, a dish of pickled gherkins and a basket of black bread. Some of the sausages seemed to consist mainly of fat and lolled pink and white and unappetising around the edge of the plate. I really wanted something hot but it was far too late to do anything about it now. I had to eat it or starve.

Gingerly, I began to sample everything and, after the initial disappointment and my distaste at the appearance of some of the items, I quite enjoyed it. Some of the things which looked awful were actually delicious provided you didn't think about them too much and, if nothing else, the whole thing was unbelievably filling. In fact, by the time I'd worked my way through three-quarters of the board, I couldn't eat any more. This was a real shame because it would have made a really good supper or even lunch the next day. I looked at it wistfully for a moment and then decided it was so much of a shame that I couldn't let it go to waste. Somehow I was going to have to take it with me or live to regret it. Surreptitiously I looked round the restaurant. The waitress was in the kitchen and I was pretty well hidden anyway so I started to make sandwiches from the leftovers. Each one I then wrapped in a paper napkin and stuffed in the capacious pockets of my overcoat until the board and the breadbasket were empty. I just hoped I didn't attract any stray dogs on the way home.

The waitress was delighted to see that everything had gone, although she remained blissfully unaware that half of it was in my overcoat pocket.

"Well that's wonderful," she said clearing the table. "You obviously enjoyed that." Then curiosity got the better of her. "Excuse me asking," she continued. "Are you a stranger here?"

"Yes I am," I answered. "I'm English."

"Ah English. How nice. On holiday?"

"No. I live here. I'm here to work. I'm an English teacher."

She was very much impressed by this gross exaggeration.

"A teacher! And you're so young! Where are you teaching?"

"In Innsbruck. In the *Bundesrealgymnasium*."

This was even better.

"In the city! A teacher in the city! How clever!" Then she grimaced slightly. "But that's a long way from here."

I found that very reassuring! I explained that I was just here for a few weeks until my room was ready in town. Having started the conversation she was curious to know all about me and my family. I liked listening to her talk with her strong country accent but found her difficult to understand. I kept up with her by catching odd words and phrase here and there and filling in the rest myself. She babbled away happily and I answered her questions as best I could, throwing in the occasional *ja* or *nein* whenever it seemed appropriate or when I couldn't find the words to say what I really wanted. She seemed to have little difficulty in understanding what I was trying to say when I did attempt a sentence and that was a great encouragement.

"Would you like a sweet, *Herr Professor*?" she asked at last, returning to the business in hand. "Or a coffee?"

Now that she knew I was a teacher I had to be addressed by the appropriate title.

"No thank you. Could I just have the bill please?"

"Of course, *Herr Professor*. Immediately."

She scurried off to fetch the bill and no doubt tell the other staff in the kitchen that there was a real English teacher from England in the restaurant. Yes really. That one over there with the old overcoat and the long hair. The one who looks like a student.

I made my way back to the flat through the cold, still blackness of the mountain night in a cheerful frame of mind, considerably perked up by the food and the conversation with the waitress. Not only did I have the prospect of a colour television and a full drinks' cabinet to look forward to for the evening, a good deal more than I'd had twenty-four hours previously, but I'd also demonstrated that I could get by with my inadequate command of German without needing Mike there to interpret for me or prompt me with vocabulary. I was beginning to believe after all that I could survive on my own up in the mountains, like some sort of linguistic commando, and, what's more, I rather liked the idea of trying it.

Chapter Seven

On Monday morning, I was roughly jerked out of my sleep by the incessant ringing of the alarm. It took me a little while to work out where I was. Then I remembered with a sinking feeling in the pit of my stomach that this was D-day. I didn't really feel up to making a good impression on people or sitting in front of classes full of staring children. My head felt as if someone had stuffed it full of cotton wool and my legs were like two jellies. In fact, it was beginning to become a habit. Two mornings out of four in Innsbruck so far I'd woken up with a hangover and I couldn't quite make up my mind whether it was my fault or the town's. This time it was down to Hans.

I'd settled down the previous evening full of good intentions. I'd found a box of pasta shells, some tomato puree and a tub of old but edible parmesan cheese in the larder and decided to save money by cooking at home and then spend a quiet evening watching television and going through my notes from Vienna before school the next day. About seven o'clock I'd decided to exercise my limited expertise in the kitchen and within half-an-hour I had something vaguely resembling an Italian pasta dish. I'd just sat down to eat when I heard a car draw up outside and someone get out. A few moments later there was a knock at the door and a key turned in the lock. I heard Hans shout:

"Anyone at home?"

"I'm in the kitchen. Come on in."

The door closed and Hans appeared.

"Hi," he said. "How goes it?"

I'd noticed he nearly always said 'how goes it' as a greeting. It was a literal translation of the standard German phrase, *Wie geht es,* which happened to work equally well in English. He saw I was eating.

"Oh sorry. I'm interrupting your dinner."

"It doesn't matter. Sit down. Do you want some?"

"No thanks. I've eaten. What is it anyway?"

I was a little embarrassed both by the frugality of the meal and the fact that I'd obviously raided his cupboards pretty thoroughly. I needn't have worried. When I'd explained what it was, Hans was only interested in the fact that I'd cooked it myself.

"That's amazing," he said. "You mean you actually know how to cook?"

"Well it wasn't difficult. I only had to boil the water."

"Yes but, I mean, you've got a sauce and everything. Where did you learn to cook?"

"I learned to cook this when I lived in France before going to university. I lived off spaghetti at the beginning when I hadn't got any money. There's nothing to it. It's no more difficult than making a cup of tea."

"Well I couldn't do it. I can't cook anything. That's the main reason I moved back home when the marriage broke up."

He moved back towards the hallway.

"Look you go on with your meal while I sort out a few things I need then we'll have a drink and a chat for a while if that's OK with you?"

I wasn't too reluctant. I didn't really feel like working and I had a lot of questions about the school and things in general that he'd be able to answer. I went back to my meal and listened to him rooting about in one of the rooms outside. I later found out he'd come to collect his long combinations and various other items of thermal underwear ready for the coming winter. Although a bit of a Music Hall joke in England, something only your Grandad wore, in Austria they were a fact of life, a sensible precaution against the bitter cold. Apparently many an elegant and fashionable ski suit on the slopes around Innsbruck covered a highly unfashionable pair of 'long johns'.

By the time I'd finished eating and washing up Hans had reappeared clutching a bottle of whisky.

"This should keep us going for a while. Or would you prefer brandy?"

"No. Whisky's fine thanks."

I waited expectantly for Hans to go and fetch some glasses and I was rather taken aback when instead he took out a jug, two mugs, some castor sugar and a handful of tea bags and put a kettle on to boil. I thought at first he just wanted a cup of tea before starting on the alcohol but he poured half the bottle of whisky into the jug, added the tea bags and spooned in some sugar. When the water boiled he poured that in as well and given it a good stir.

"That'll keep us warm," he said putting it on the table and sitting down. "A nice hot toddy."

"I hope a Scotsman never sees you do that," I answered.

"Why not? I've seen them put hot water and sugar in whisky in the mountains. We're all alike really, mountain people. You do what you have to to keep warm. That's all that matters. We call it *Jägertee* but we normally stick rum in it." He poured me a mugful. "Go on. Try it."

I gave it a tentative sip and felt it burn its way down and start a fire in my stomach. After the initial shock it was surprisingly good.

"That's not bad. If nothing else it would certainly keep you warm."

"You imagine drinking that at a little mountain hut after a morning's skiing, sitting on a wooden bench in the open air, the snow clean and crisp around you, a few pairs of skis lined up at the side with the poles stuck into the ground, people whooshing past enjoying it too much to stop, your face burning in the cold. It's wonderful. There's nothing like it."

"It might make skiing a bit difficult afterwards."

"Not really. You do yourself a lot less harm when you fall. Are you a skier?"

"I don't think 'skier' is quite the right word somehow. I have done some skiing but not much. Just a week in France on the nursery slopes. But it was great. That's one of the reasons I came here, hoping to learn to ski properly."

"Good. That's important learning properly. Too many people get hurt because they don't know what they're doing. I tell you what, when the season comes I'll take you up and teach you. I'm a state-qualified instructor."

"That'd be great. Thanks very much."

"We'll go up to Mutters. There's a good, long, easy run up there. We could probably spend the whole morning on it."

At the time, of course, I didn't quite appreciate the magnitude of what he was offering me. Becoming a state-qualified instructor was almost as difficult as becoming an international. Really good skiers could make it as regional instructors but to become state-qualified you had to be outstanding. And Hans was outstanding both as a skier and as an instructor but at the time I didn't know enough about Austrian skiing to understand what a big favour he was doing me. I was just pleased that he was interested enough to want to teach me.

The first pot of toddy slipped down nicely as we talked and I had begun to feel pleasantly warm and mellow and only slightly drunk.

"Why don't we finish the bottle?" Hans said when the pot was empty. "It doesn't seem right to leave it half full like this."

"Remember tomorrow's my first day at school. I don't want to turn up with a hangover."

"You won't have to do much. Anyway you'll be alright. We're only drinking it slowly."

I didn't really need much encouragement and so he made a second pot the same as the first.

The effects of the toddy seemed to be exponential and by the time we were halfway through the second pot the conversation had begun to get out of hand. I'd started to experience serious problems with my mouth, which would no longer respond to signals from my brain, and Hans had lapsed into maudlin and largely incoherent reflections on the failure of his marriage. It had got worse and worse as the teapot emptied until finally I was just sitting grinning moronically as Hans wittered on about wasting the best years of his life. He only stopped when he noticed his mug was empty. He picked up the pot and turned it upside down over the table until the teabags slithered out in a soggy heap.

"It's empty," he said, blinking vacantly, his hand swaying from side to side as it clutched the pot. "Need more." He dropped the pot sideways down on the table and unsteadily got to his feet.

"Need more whisky," he slurred.

Even in my befuddled state I realised that this was not a good idea but I no longer had any control over my mouth. By the time I'd managed to make any sound at all, Hans had staggered off towards the lounge.

It was quite some time before it occurred to me that a simple trip into the next room shouldn't take more than a few moments and a further five minutes passed while I tried to focus on the problem of what to do next. Then with a superhuman effort I managed to stand up and waited for the room to stop spinning round. Once I'd reached a certain level of stability, I left the kitchen and reeled off into the lounge.

Hans was nowhere to be seen and I thought at first he must have gone to bed. I attempted to call his name but my vocal chords were by now totally paralysed. I'd just decided to go to bed when I suddenly noticed a pair of feet sticking out from behind the settee. I staggered over and found the rest of Hans sprawled out on the floor in front of the cocktail cabinet, a full bottle of whisky in his hand. He was fast asleep and snoring quietly to himself. There didn't seem much point in trying to wake him and he was far too large for me to move on my own so I made my way unsteadily back to my room, just grateful to have avoided the second bottle.

I found Hans downstairs in the kitchen making coffee.

"I was just going to wake you," he said as I appeared. "Want some coffee?"

"Yes please. And a blood transfusion."

"Hangover huh?"

"I feel like death warmed up."

He liked that.

"That's great. I've never heard that one before. It's a common idiom is it?"

"It is for me. I seem to feel like it all the time here."

A few months later, remembering its effect on Hans, I used the same phrase to another English teacher at the school. Unfortunately, his best friend had been killed the previous day in a skiing accident. It didn't quite get the reaction I'd expected.

"Come on," said Hans, "teach me some more."

"Oh God. It's seven o'clock in the morning, Hans, and I'm dying. Be reasonable."

"Oh come on. Just one more."

I sighed heavily.

"Alright. You see these." I pointed to my swollen, bloodshot eyes. "These are eyes like pissholes in the snow."

This was even better.

"That's fantastic," he said excitedly. He repeated it over and over again chuckling to himself.

"How come you're so bright and cheerful this morning? By rights you ought to feel worse than me."

"I never get hangovers. I don't know why. I woke up on the settee feeling right as rain."

"How did you get to the settee?"

He was puzzled.

"I presume I decided to sleep there because you had the bedroom."

"No. You decided to sleep on the floor behind the settee."

I explained how I had found him the night before.

"I suppose I must have moved under my own steam during the night. God, how embarrassing." He gave me a sheepish smile. "I guess the whisky must have got to me before I got to it."

Hans drove me into school and despite the rush hour traffic we arrived at the school with minutes to spare. As we turned into the staff car park, I noticed to my horror that the playground and all the entrances were packed with children. As I got out of the car, I was the immediate focus of attention and I could feel every gaze fixed on me, the pupils nudging each other and whispering, speculating about who I might be. By the time we reached the haven of the main entrance, I had flushed a bright red, acutely embarrassed by the attention of several hundred children.

"Don't worry," said Hans as he walked me up to the staffroom, obviously aware of my discomfort, "you'll soon just become another part of the furniture."

Entering the packed staffroom was almost as bad as running the gauntlet in the playground. I felt myself going red again but this time I was literally saved by the bell which announced the beginning of classes in five minutes. Most of the staff began to gather up their books for the first lesson and lost interest but one man, with large twinkling blue eyes and a bushy black beard, stayed seated at a table, puffing contentedly at a cigarette, watching me and smiling quietly. Hans led me over to him.

"*Grüss Di, Reiner*," he said in his thick Tyrolean accent. "Here's your new assistant, safe and sound but a little hungover."

"*Danke Hans*," he growled. "You can leave him to me now."

He held out his hand and said in perfectly unaccented English:

"Welcome on board, Iain. Come and sit down. I'll try and talk quietly."

"I'll see you later," said Hans. "I'd better go off and teach."

He left us alone in the virtually deserted staffroom and I sat down opposite Reiner.

"Been indulging in the local spirits, have we?" he said with a wry smile. "I like that in an assistant provided you still make it to work on time. What was it? Schnapps?"

"No. Half a bottle of whisky. Hans decided to teach me about *Jägertee*."

He laughed.

"Well we'll have to do it properly sometime with *Stroh* rum and schnapps. Sorry I wasn't here on Friday. I had a National Council meeting in Graz. Still it looks like Reitenberger's been looking after you. Are you alright up there?"

"I'm fine. I've got a place sorted out in town at the end of the month so it's only for a few weeks."

"Good. I'm glad you can look after yourself." He grinned. "I'm not much good at playing nursemaid. Still we'll see if we can make it a bit easier for you. There must be someone who drives in from your way. Maybe we can sort out a lift in or something."

"Thanks. The bus isn't very convenient. It only comes in as far as the station."

"Right. I'll see what I can do. Now to business." He indicated the pile of papers in front of him. "I'm afraid there are a few boring formalities to sort out first. We'll get those out of the way and then go and talk about your timetable over a beer. Although in your delicate condition you'd probably better stick to coffee. Let's do the paperwork first."

I was beginning to feel quite inferior at the Austrians' command of

English and Reiner's was the best I'd come across yet. Hans spoke it well but the slight trace of an Austrian accent was always there. Reiner, on the other hand, had a perfect Mid-Atlantic English accent with no trace of Austrian at all. As I got to know him I became more and more impressed. His accent, vocabulary and grammar were so good that I constantly had to remind myself that he was Austrian and not English. Only very occasionally did he make a mistake, normally with a difficult idiom and, more often than not, he corrected himself immediately. I knew I'd never be able to speak German that well. I just didn't have the ear for it.

"Now you probably think this is a waste of time, and you may well be right," continued Reiner. "But the first thing I have to have is a written acceptance of the rules. It's legally binding so you need to take it seriously. I mean if you were a communist infiltrator or a rapist you would obviously stand up and tell me now rather than sign a legally binding document, wouldn't you?"

I started to speak but he stopped me.

"It's alright. You don't really need to answer that. It was a joke. Even if you are I don't want to know. What is not a joke, however, is paragraph four relating to fraternisation. Fraternisation is, of course, a euphemism for humping. You obviously don't hold any outrageous political or religious views because they would have checked before giving you a job in Austria. On the other hand I assume you're normal and like women. For all I know they may have checked that too. But fraternisation with the female pupils is right out unless you want to go through the rest of your life without fraternisation equipment. You can have the whole female population of the University for all I care; in fact, I might even join you. You can even screw your way through all the female members of staff, in which case I definitely won't, but if you so much as lay a finger on one of the girls, I will personally remove your fraternisation equipment before the law gets to you. Don't even be seen outside school hours with them in case rumours start. You will be tempted because some of them are gorgeous and there's always a little bit of teasing goes on in class but for your own good and, more importantly mine, God help me, control yourself. OK?"

I read it through quickly and signed it. There was no way I was going to refuse anyway. We'd been warned in Vienna that we had no choice.

"Good," said Reiner. He picked up a second form. "This is a notification of your conditions of employment. It says that you understand what you're here to do. You're required to work twelve hours a week which is sixteen periods of forty-five minutes. I've actually allocated you seventeen one week and thirteen the next on a fortnightly cycle. You could refuse to accept that, of course, but I wouldn't advise it. It's a pretty fair timetable as you'll see. In return, you get paid some exorbitant sum to finance your debauchery while you're here - usually drink, women and smuggling trips to Italy. I doubt if you'll get anything before the end of November because it takes time to get you into the system but feel free to borrow anything you need to tide you over. Alright? Just read it and sign it."

He waited patiently while I read it through. It was the first time I'd actually seen my salary and I was impressed. I was to get 6750 schillings a month, about £250. It was a colossal sum to penniless student and after paying my rent, I'd still have enough to live very comfortably in Innsbruck. I only wished I could have it now. I signed the form and handed it back.

"Right and this is your timetable," said Reiner, pulling out a large folded sheet of paper. "Memorise it, then swallow it."

I took it and stretched it out on the table.

"Now in Austria," he continued, "we work six days a week but I thought the shock might be too much for your delicate English constitution so I've given you every Saturday off. Since you'll probably want to go away for weekends I've also given you Fridays off as well. And once a fortnight you get Wednesday free so you can go skiing or spend all day in bed. The rest of the time you'll have to work bloody hard but I think it's worth it and anyway we only teach until one, apart from a few special classes. They won't involve you so you'll have every afternoon to yourself."

It was a brilliant timetable, better than anything I'd expected and I was extremely grateful to Reiner.

"This is great," I said. "Thanks very much. You obviously went to a lot of trouble over it."

Reiner shrugged his shoulders.

"No big deal. It doesn't make any difference to the school how you do your classes and it wasn't very difficult to arrange it that way. I was an assistant once and it makes a big difference if you can go away for three days at the weekend. You can see and do so much more."

"When do I start?"

"Well for the first few weeks you get to take it easy. You just sit in the classroom and observe. It gives you a chance to see how we operate and get a feel for the level of the kids in each of the classes."

I nodded.

"Bud Ryan and Hans mentioned that I had to spectate for two weeks."

"It's no great hardship. You should find it quite interesting with any luck. Today you might as well come into my first lesson with me and then we can pick up your actual timetable from there and give you a chance to get used to it. And remember punctuality is important over here. Even in my exalted position I can't afford to be late for a class. The same applies to you in your far from exalted position, even though there'll always be a teacher with the class to cover for you. If for any reason you can't make it in, phone up and let me know. Even if it's only to tell us you've got sausage poisoning."

"Why sausage poisoning?" I asked.

Reiner grinned.

"Sausage poisoning is the standard excuse here when you want a day off," he explained. "It's like saying you've got the flu or a bad cold in England."

He pulled yet more papers out onto the desk.

"Just one more then," said Reiner. "This is for your personal details; address in Innsbruck, next of kin in case you die of alcohol poisoning and bank account number. You probably haven't got one of those yet."

"What here?"

"Well that would seem best unless you want to be paid direct into a secret Swiss bank account. You'll need to go and open one and let Frau Hinckle, the school secretary, have the number as soon as possible. Don't waste too much time before you do that, it's important."

He gave me the final form and I filled in the details and signed it.

"Great. That's all the paperwork out of the way. We just need to pop in and see the boss, and then we can go and have that drink.

Chapter Eight

It was a weird experience walking into an Austrian classroom for the first time, following at Reiner's heels like a little dog. My entrance caused an immediate stir of excitement among the thirty or so pupils in the room, a mixed group aged around fifteen. There was a buzz of excited whispering and frantic nudging of neighbours until they were roughly silenced by Reiner. They obviously felt that today's lesson was going to be something really special.

The class in question was 5d, Reiner's first class of the day.

"You'll like this lot," Reiner had said as we'd hurried down the corridor on our return from the coffee shop. "They're thick as four short planks but they've got a certain raw, uncultured charm. They'll love you."

I spent the rest of the day trying to work out whether that was a subtle insult or not.

"This is Herr Moss," said Reiner, "he's our new English assistant. He'll be with us for the whole year so you'll be seeing quite a lot of him."

The expression on their faces clearly showed that they were perfectly happy at this prospect and I was flattered.

"Can someone bring him the empty chair from the back?"

Half the class jumped to their feet and a minor skirmish ensued as the first group to reach the chair fought for the honour of bringing it to me. At last the victor, red-faced and panting, his face wreathed in smiles, dragged the chair to the front and plonked it at my feet like a dog fetching a stick.

"For you, *Herr 'fessor*," he announced proudly and swaggered back to his desk.

"Thank you," I said and sat down behind Reiner who opened the book on his desk.

"Right," he said, "now let's get down to some work. Using the passive..."

As the kids worked, answering Reiner's questions in faltering English and making notes in their exercise books I could see them throwing surreptitious glances in my direction, and smiling knowingly at each other. They were obviously convinced that this was just a preamble on Reiner's part, a little tease to build up the suspense and excitement before I was called upon to step forward and do my act. This was going to be something really special, they could tell. I could almost touch the anticipation and excitement in the room.

Reiner finished reviewing the previous lesson and moved on to new material, asking questions in English, throwing insults in German and writing on the blackboard. The class worked on, still watching me and waiting for the big moment, the air of anticipation slowly building to a climax.

After twenty minutes or so had elapsed a hint of impatience appeared in the surreptitious glances and the looks to their friends tacitly asked 'why doesn't he get on with it?' The excitement was still there but I could feel it wavering as doubts about my entertainment value slowly began to creep in.

As the end of the lesson approached, they were still staring at me expectantly but now with a hint of anxiety on their faces and when the bell finally rang and I'd still made no move and I trooped out again behind Reiner, thirty pairs of puzzled and disappointed eyes followed me through the door. I could hear the buzz of a dozen conversations break out in our wake and I imagined them telling each other what a real dead-loss I'd turned out to be.

My next lesson was much more interesting. The teacher was Frau Doktor Grindl, a very imposing lady of about forty-five with immaculately coiffured hair piled high on her head and gold butterfly wing glasses perched on her nose. I was a little wary of her at first especially since Reiner's last words before he introduced me were:

"Right, St. George, come and meet the dragon."

In the event, although a real tartar when angry and a strict disciplinarian in the classroom, Else Grindl never treated me with anything but immense kindness. Unlike Hans and Reiner, she addressed me in German, except inside the classroom which came as something of a relief. I'd started to wonder whether I was ever going to get the chance to speak German at school.

"I know you're not meant to do anything for the first couple of weeks," she said as we set off down the corridor, "but, if you don't mind, I would like you just to say a few words to this class. They're very good at English and it would so please them to talk to a real native speaker for a change."

I was perfectly happy with this.

"I don't mind at all," I said, "I felt stupid just sitting there doing nothing in Reiner's class."

"Good. I'll just run through their homework with them and then you can have a few minutes before I start on any new work."

The class was 7a and they very soon became my favourite pupils. They were older than the first class, around seventeen, lively and intelligent, with a real interest in England and the English. They were all perfectly capable of holding a conversation in the language and, more importantly, were willing to make the effort to do so. Unlike 5d, they didn't have long to wait. Else quickly ran through the previous day's work, questioned them on what they'd been set to learn at home and then handed over to me.

"This is Mr. Moss, our new English Assistant. I've asked him to spend a few moments telling you about himself and where he comes from. Please listen very carefully and try and remember some of the words and phrases he uses so that we can talk about them later." She turned to me and said quietly: "Right Iain, they're all yours."

I was a little nervous standing up in front of a class again to teach but not as much as I'd expected. After all, only two weeks before I'd been doing it every day as part of the summer school I'd taught. In fact, I was more nervous about performing in front of a professional teacher. I'd given it some thought while Else was teaching and decided that, if I just talked, it would probably be boring. So I'd decided to make it a sort of guessing game instead.

"You probably think," I began, "that just because I'm called the English Assistant I must come from England. But of course, if you think about it carefully, you'll realise that that isn't necessarily true. In fact, there are lots of other countries I could come from where English is spoken as the native language. What I want you to do is tell me what you know about those countries and then decide which one you think I come from. Does everybody understand?"

There were a few nods of assent from the class so I presumed that I must be getting through.

At first they were rather shy and I found it difficult to get very much out of them, even the names of the English speaking countries. All my questions and prompts were just met with stony silence. In the end, I went through the list myself, just to get them started, and wrote them up on the board. This was a sign of real desperation on my part because the one thing I always tried to avoid while teaching was the blackboard. My handwriting is appalling at the best of times but on a blackboard it looks like a child of six has been practising the alphabet. It wasn't long, however, before they warmed up a bit and started to take part and soon they even seemed to be enjoying the novelty of the game. After all anything was better than studying grammar.

We did a quick whistle stop tour of the world, stopping off at South Africa, Australia, New Zealand, Canada and America on the way and talking about the national characteristics of each country's inhabitants. We had a lot of fun swapping prejudices and misconceptions. I explained how we saw everything in Australia as being upside down and that the people were descended from British convicts and that the Americans were brash and noisy, given to wearing outrageous clothing and that we were two countries 'divided by a common language'. Having eliminated these, we came down to Great Britain and Ireland and again went through the process of identifying racial characteristics and airing racial prejudices. I told them some Irish jokes and they were fascinated because they had almost identical jokes in German but about the people of Burgenland, a region on the Austrian border with Hungary. We talked about Welsh singing and rugby, Scottish kilts and whisky and finally ended up with England again. This gave them a real chance to air their prejudices. According to the Austrians, all English people wore bowler hats and pinstripe suits, were cold, unemotional and terribly, terribly polite, spent every afternoon drinking tea and ruined every meat dish with mint sauce. By way of retaliation I told them that all Austrians ate nothing but sausages, were very fat and walked around the whole time in Lederhosen with skis over their shoulders. That certainly got them talking.

I eventually gave in and agreed that I was English, which I'm sure they'd known from the start, but I wasn't going to let them off the hook totally just yet.

"That still doesn't tell you very much, does it?" I said. "England's a big place. Tell me about the different counties and the big towns. I want you to guess which part of England I come from."

Inevitably, the only big town they could come up with was London but they seemed to know it almost as well as if they'd lived there. Most English language teaching books devoted several chapters to the capital and they could all direct me around the West End, describe Piccadilly Circus in minute detail and even discourse knowledgeably about the tube system. I wasn't happy, though, that they seemed to view England as London with a few minor towns and villages thrown in for good measure.

"Come on now," I said, "there are lots of very large cities in England besides London. You must be able to name some of them."

Unfortunately, they didn't get a chance because as soon as I'd asked the question the bell rang. I'd taken up almost the whole lesson without realizing it.

I apologised profusely to Else on the way back to the staffroom for wasting her lesson, but she was obviously delighted.

"Don't be silly," she said. "That was marvellous. They were really involved at the end. And, more importantly, they were all talking. I'm quite sure it did them far more good than forty-five minutes of grammar with me. Well done."

I felt really good after that and the feeling of euphoria stayed with me all through the next lesson, 2e with Reiner, in which I was yet again ignored for forty-five minutes, much to the bewilderment and disappointment of the class. My last period of the day was with 4b, presided over by a diminutive probationary teacher called Suzi. She was a shy elfin figure of about twenty-five with short auburn hair and large green eyes. She'd come to teaching late and this was her *Probejahr* at the end of which she would be assessed for a permanent post and she was still very nervous and unsure of herself. She was also acutely self-conscious about her English. All through the first part of the lesson she kept glancing across at me as she spoke as if she was afraid that I was going to jump up and correct her every few minutes. In fact, her English was good accurate textbook stuff spoken with a typical 'BBC' accent and precise pronunciation. It was a real giveaway that she was foreign, compared, for example, with Hans or Reiner, but that was actually unimportant unless she was planning to take up work as an undercover agent.

Halfway through the lesson she asked me whether I would like to talk to the class for a while so I got up and went into the same routine I'd used earlier with Else. It's always a mistake to use a good trick twice and I had a lot more trouble the second time. The pupils were younger and less capable and I had to work very hard to keep the conversation going until the bell rang. It wasn't a disaster and I did manage to get them talking in the end, if somewhat reluctantly, but it certainly wasn't the success it had been the first time. I learnt more than the kids in the sense that it was my first real experience of moving between groups of greatly differing ability. Since my timetable covered the whole school from first year to eighth, I was going to have to learn to alter my style considerably between classes. Suzi made sure the time wasn't wasted anyway. All the time I was talking, she sat making notes on the vocabulary I was using and I guessed she would go back over anything the class hadn't understood in a later lesson.

One thing had struck me forcibly that first morning about Austrian teaching methods. Every lesson, even with the very junior pupils, had been conducted entirely in English. Very occasionally it was necessary for the teacher to translate a difficult word or phrase but it was avoided wherever possible. They started with known vocabulary and then slowly introduced new words and ideas in context so that pupils could steadily improve their grasp of the language without having to keep translating back to German in their heads. It was a way of avoiding what was technically known as 'mother tongue interference', so that students could learn a foreign language naturally rather than artificially by continuous reference to their own. No language translates directly into another and traditional teaching methods, like those used in my own school in England, left pupils speaking a foreign language heavily shaped by the grammar and idioms of their own. It was the first time I'd seen the method in use and I was highly impressed. The standard of English in the classes spoke for itself.

Suzi's class marked the end of my first day's teaching and I left the school and hurried off to the Old Town to meet Mike. When I arrived there he was not alone. Standing with him was Maurice, one of the French assistants based in Innsbruck, who we'd met briefly in Vienna. As I approached Mike said to me in German:

"Hi, Iain. Maurice works part-time in the same school as me. How about that?"

Since we'd both known this already and discussed it at length, I assumed that Mike was just warning me not to speak English. As usual I was annoyed and frustrated at having to speak German when there was so much I wanted to say about the things that had happened since we last met. Not only would I have difficulty putting it all over in German but also Maurice was a virtual stranger and I doubted if he'd be particularly interested in my exploits so far. But we'd already agreed that we needed more contact with the French assistants to stop us speaking English all the time so I gritted my teeth manfully and greeted Maurice in German. He acknowledged me with a little bow of his head and we set off towards the nearer of the two refectories up on Innrain which ran alongside the river.

Maurice was a most un-French looking Frenchman. He had short-cropped curly blond hair, a very pale complexion and blue eyes covered by large horn-rimmed glasses. He was thin to the point of being emaciated. He came from Dijon in eastern France and spoke very good accurate German with a strong Swiss accent. I hadn't been struck in Vienna by a sparkling vivacious personality and I wasn't any more impressed at this second meeting.

The *Mensa* was a large rather Spartan cafeteria affair on the first floor of one of the university buildings. All along one side there was a series of serving areas backing on to the kitchen, each dispensing a separate part of the meal, divided off from the rest of the room by a rail just like a self-service restaurant, which of course it was. Packed into the remaining floor space were vinyl covered dining tables, seating four, six or eight people. According to Maurice, further up the road in the basement of the main university building was a smaller more intimate *Mensa* where the food and the atmosphere were a good deal better, but it got crowded very quickly at lunchtime being right in the heart of the university and it was usually hard to get a table.

The large *Mensa* was virtually empty when we arrived, the main rush being over, and there was no shortage of tables and no queues. We took a tray each and walked the gauntlet of the serving areas. At the first we were given a bowl of thin vegetable soup, at the second a plate of goulash and boiled potatoes, then a dish of beetroot salad and finally a bowl of fruit in syrup. For this we were charged twenty schillings - about sixty pence.

Conversation during the meal was very stilted. I was inhibited by having to speak German and Maurice didn't seem to be much of a conversationalist in any language. It was left to poor Mike to do his best to keep things going but it was an uphill struggle. Maurice was very much an academic and his only conversational gambits were attempts to discuss our studies or works of German literature to which we both responded unenthusiastically. We were both primarily linguists and although we enjoyed literature we weren't really into dissecting it syllable by syllable.

"Well," said Mike eventually, desperately trying to get some kind of reasonable conversation going, "we've all had a morning at school. What do you think of the way they teach?"

I had a lot to say about that but none of the vocabulary in German to say it. We both looked at Maurice.

"In my view," he answered ponderously, wiping his mouth with a serviette, "they don't teach enough literature."

We waited expectantly for him to continue but, just as slowly, he went back to his food.

"I think it's very good," I said weakly, trying to hold my end up.

Mike looked at me, willing me to continue but my mind went blank.

"Why do you think they should teach more literature, Maurice?" he asked after a long silence.

Again we waited as the Frenchman wiped his mouth and formulated an answer.

"What is the purpose of learning a language if it's not to

appreciate the beauty of its literature?" he said at last.

I knew Mike had strong views, as I did, on the importance of spoken language and I waited with interest for his response.

"How about communicating with its people?" he asked and I clearly heard the underlying note of sarcasm.

Again there was a delay before Maurice responded.

"One can do that quite adequately with grunts and signs like the primitives did. The only real purpose of language is to record man's finer thoughts and allow them to be communicated to those able to appreciate them."

I began to search desperately in my mind for the German equivalent of 'claptrap' but Mike got there long before me.

"I'm sorry but that's rubbish. The main purpose of any language is to speak it. That's what keeps it alive and growing. If you just confine it to a written form it dies. Like Latin."

"There's nothing dead about Latin. The literature is still vibrant and alive."

"No it isn't. It's historically interesting but it's certainly not alive. Nobody's writing about modern day events and problems in Latin. The body of literature's not growing and contributing to the way we understand the world."

"Well you're studying Swedish and Swedish literature's already dead and they're still writing it."

Things got very nasty after that and Mike and Maurice were soon at each other's throats, all academic objectivity right out of the window. I just sat back and watched the fireworks, frustrated that I hadn't got the command of German to join in. Not that it mattered. Mike was taking the stand I would have taken myself, almost, except that emotion was driving him way over the top. They argued violently for some minutes and then suddenly, almost at the same moment, they seemed to realize that if they didn't stop they were going to open up wounds that might never heal. They lapsed into silence and we finished the main course without another word, heads down over our food. Eventually Maurice pushed away his dessert and stood up.

"I think I'll go over to the University library for the afternoon. I've got some work to do there. I'll see you both another time."

We watched him gather up his things and leave the building. Mike looked at his soggy tinned-fruit swimming in syrup and pushed it away.

"I don't fancy this much," he said. "Let's go and have a cake somewhere."

After a coffee and a cake that cost us more than the whole meal at the *Mensa*, I walked Mike back up to the technical college where he had an afternoon class.

"I think you did rather better than me in the timetable stakes," said Mike rather glumly as we headed off towards the college. "I wouldn't mind going home now."

It was ironic that, two days ago, I'd been jealous of the progress Mike had made and now, here he was, jealous of me. Since we each only had the other's experience for comparison, I suppose it was inevitable. The other man's grass always looks greener, but in fact the brown patches are just in different places!

"Well look on the bright side," I answered. "At least you get lots of free periods. It'll give you a chance to get to know the staff."

"Like Maurice, I suppose. I bet his idea of a fun night out is a reading of medieval German poetry. "

"Well even that might be worth it," I said laughing. "Just to meet the mysterious Mlle. X. He's the only one who knows where she lives or what she looks like, remember?"

We knew from Vienna that there was a second French Assistant in Innsbruck, a girl, but we hadn't managed to meet her during the induction course.

"She'd better be something pretty damn special then, that's all I can say."

"Well who knows? She could be the key to our whole social life. Witty, vivacious, lots of nubile Austrian friends. Just what we're looking for."

"Or she could be another academic with horn-rimmed glasses and lots of female friends all just like Maurice."

"Well in that case we'll just have to cultivate an interest in medieval German poetry. Won't we?"

This time he laughed.

"Yes, why not. Anyway I hear that some of it is really quite erotic."

I left him at the school gates and walked back into town. I had some shopping to do. I couldn't face another meal of pasta.

Chapter Nine

My clearest memory of those first weeks in Innsbruck is of blistered aching feet. I don't think I have ever walked so much in my life. From the first walk down the steep, stony, mud-slippery track in the morning to the even more strenuous return journey up that same track at night, I seemed to be permanently on my feet.

As I'd feared the worst days were those when I wanted to stay in town to see a film or go out for a meal in the evening. At first I tried to do this as often as possible since it seemed a waste to spend a lot of time on my own watching television, but it was hard on my feet. Killing time for several hours is a demoralising process and I would just wander aimlessly round the town, already tired from the early start in the morning, until I was literally fit to drop. I couldn't afford to spend much time in coffee shops so, when I finally couldn't walk any further, I would just drop down on a park bench somewhere. In the end, I even developed the knack of being able to fall asleep for a while, only to wake up feeling ten times worse with the added problem of a crick in my neck. Fortunately it never occurred to me to wonder what someone from the school would have thought if they'd seen the new English assistant sprawled across a park bench, dead to the world, like some wino or tramp.

The biggest casualty of all was the weekly volleyball club held at the school on Tuesdays. It was obviously a great way of getting to know the younger members of staff and I really wanted to go. Unfortunately, it was a turn-up-if-you-feel-like-it kind of event involving no prior commitment. Each Tuesday I carried my sports gear into work, determined to turn up at seven, come what may, got fed up with the long afternoon ramble and went home. I'd virtually resigned myself to waiting until I moved into town when circumstances conspired to get me to volleyball at last and in so doing nearly ruined my first trip out of Innsbruck.

In the middle of my second week in Axams Hans buttonholed me at school one day and introduced me to a short dark man in his late twenties called Viktor.

"Viktor teaches religion and philosophy," said Hans. "He and his wife have just moved into a house up in one of the villages beyond Axams. He has to pass through there every day on his way to work and he thought he might be able to give you a lift some days."

I was delighted. Reiner had obviously passed the word round that I could do with some help.

"I get to Axams about twenty past seven," said Viktor shaking my hand. "If nothing else it'll give you that little bit longer in bed every morning."

That suited me down to the ground.

"Thanks very much. That'll make life a lot easier. The only problem is my timetable. I don't work every day, you see, and it's not the same every week. I'm not sure how we would arrange it."

"No problem," said Viktor. "If you're not at the bus stop on the main road by seven-twenty, I'll just assume you're not going in."

"That's good. Then even if I oversleep or I'm sick or something I won't make you late."

The system worked very well and I began to feel a good deal better for the extra sleep and the more relaxed journey to work each day. As an added bonus, Viktor and I hit it off together right from the start. He couldn't speak any foreign languages, apart from a little schoolboy English, and was fascinated by my clumsy attempts at speaking German. He used to like to help me when I was finding it difficult to express something and teach me new words and phrases. It gave him tremendous pleasure, days later, to hear me use in conversation something he himself had taught me.

One morning as we were driving down to work Viktor said:

"There's another *Wandertag* on Wednesday. I'm taking my class and another one over to South Tyrol and I was wondering if you'd like to come with us."

South Tyrol was in the Northern part of Italy just over the border from Austria. Up until the First World War it had been part of the Austrian Tyrol but had been ceded to Italy as part of the peace treaty. It was a large prosperous wine-growing area and its loss was still deeply felt among the people in the Austrian Tyrol. As a consequence it had become something of a tradition to go over late in the year to sample the new red wine.

"It should be a good day out," continued Viktor. "We can drink some red wine, eat lots of spaghetti and go for a long ramble through the hills. There's some beautiful countryside down there and they all speak German so there's no language problem. It'll only cost you twenty schillings towards the coach plus whatever you spend while you're there, of course. How about it?"

Wild horses wouldn't have stopped me.

"Thanks very much. I'd love to go."

"Great. I let you have all the details when we get to school."

I spent the rest of the week really looking forward to the trip. It was an unexpected stroke of luck being able to notch up a trip to Italy so early in my stay, made all the sweeter by Mike's obvious envy when I told him. I decided it would be an ideal opportunity to send home all the postcards I'd been meaning to write since I arrived, giving them some added spice by posting them from Italy. I might as well make everybody else envious as well.

The day before the trip I ducked out of volleyball as usual and went straight back up to the village after lunch. I was beginning to like living in Axams. It had a charm all of its own and, in stark contrast to cosmopolitan Innsbruck, a foreigner was something of a novelty among the villagers. At first I'd found this quite difficult to handle. After lunch on my first day in Axams I'd taken a walk down into the village to have a look round. I got something of a surprise when I reached the centre of the village itself. I'd expected it to be deserted on a Sunday afternoon but instead it was full of people, laughing and talking and strolling about. There were even street traders there with small wooden stalls selling hot punch, sweet nougat and trinkets for the children. The villagers were dressed as I'd always imagined they should be; the men in their magnificent green and grey embroidered dress suits with feathers in their hats, the boys in lederhosen and the women and girls in dainty blue and white *Dirndl* dresses with flowers in their hair. It was almost too perfect to be true like something that should only happen on the set of the 'Sound of Music'. At the time I'd thought I was just lucky and that I'd chanced upon a saint's day festival or a village celebration but, in fact, it happened every week, year in year out. It was just a way of celebrating Sunday, a day of rest away from the fields. It was a chance to put away their dirty working clothes and dress up in their Sunday best. In the past, it had probably also been an occasion for showing off one's marriageable daughters to the local bachelors and finding them husbands. Something similar probably happened in villages all over Austria on a Sunday. In fact, as I'd discovered later, it even happened in Innsbruck to a lesser extent with numerous families dressing up in traditional dress and taking to the streets. At the time, however, I'd felt privileged to be watching what I believed to be a unique occasion.

I'd also felt alarmingly conspicuous. Ironically I was the one dressed strangely not them and I also stood out as someone they didn't recognise. I could see the question marks appearing in people's eyes as I walked by them and the excited, whispered conversations behind me once I'd passed. I'd wanted to stay out walking and enjoying the festive atmosphere but in the end all the attention became a strain. I'd taken one quick walk round the village, just to get my bearings and then retreated back to the flat. After a few days, however, we'd got a bit more used to each other. I was seen regularly at the Bus Stop in the morning and shopping in the village in the afternoon and once I'd started chatting to the local shopkeepers, all of whom, just like the waitress in the restaurant, were desperate to know all about me, I was no longer a strange object of curiosity and people would instead greet me with a polite *Grüss Gott* when they passed me in the street. I still hadn't managed to summon up the courage, though, to drop in to one of the local inns one night for a drink. I suspected that if I did it regularly I would eventually get to know a few people but I could imagine the embarrassment of sitting there all on my own the first couple of times not knowing anyone and I kept putting it off. I convinced myself that since I was only there for a few weeks, there was no real point in trying too hard but I knew full well that it was just a rather weak excuse.

That Tuesday, I did some shopping in the village and chatted to the friendly middle-aged lady who ran the grocery shop and then settled down at home for the rest of the day. At about five-thirty, however, I heard a car draw up outside and a few moments later a key turned in the lock and Hans did his 'anyone at home' routine.

"I'm in the lounge," I shouted. "Come on in."

I had had a sneaking feeling that I might see Hans that evening, I'd made use of the afternoon at home to wash my clothes in his washing machine and the last batch was now in the tumble drier. Whenever I was engaged in anything even vaguely domestic, Hans always seemed to turn up. Although he always claimed to be amazingly impressed at how practical and domesticated I was, I'd begun to wonder if, given his background, he might have started to find it all a bit odd for a man. This time, fortunately, he didn't notice because the machine switched itself off without him actually setting foot in the kitchen.

"Hi," he said coming into the lounge, "how goes it? I thought I'd just pop in and see how you were. What are you doing tonight?"

"Nothing much. Why?"

"I just thought it would be nice if you came and played volleyball. You seemed quite keen when I told you about it and I thought that perhaps you'd been put off by the distance and not having anyone to go with."

I decided not to tell him about the long afternoons walking the streets and being too fed up to go usually. I didn't want him to feel that his flat was inadequate in any way.

"That's great," I said, "I'd love to go, thanks. Hey, why don't you have dinner with me first? I've got plenty of bread, cheese and sausage."

"No it's OK," said Hans. "I've got a better idea. I'll take you for a typical Austrian supper. It'll be good for your education. Get your sports gear and we'll go."

A typical Austrian supper turned out to be a two stage affair. For the first we needed a restaurant and after parking the car behind the Old Town, Hans took me to a place next to the famous 'Golden Roof' called, with breathtaking originality, *Goldenes Dachl* - 'The Golden Roof'. It was part of the same chain as 'Moby Dick's' but a good deal more tasteful, despite the name, and with a much better menu. In fact, it offered a wide range of regional specialities which is why we were there.

Inside, it was an old Tirolean *Bierstüberl* with large wooden tables and hard wooden benches. It looked authentic and I guessed it was an original Inn which had been taken over and preserved virtually intact by the new management. We sat down and Hans ordered something which sounded like goulash. I liked goulash but I was a bit surprised. Served with potatoes and dumplings it was going to sit in our stomachs like a lead weight while we played volleyball. When the waitress came back, however, she was carrying two little bowls and a basket of black bread.

"This," said Hans, as she placed the rich brown liquid in front of us, "is goulash soup, a famous local speciality. They do it rather well here. Try it and tell me what you think."

I did as I was asked and it was delicious, rich and spicy, sequined with golden bubbles of fat and generously laden with little cubes of meat and potato. Eaten with slices of the heavy black bread it also looked like it would be quite filling.

"I hope you're not planning on ordering a main course after this," I said only half-joking. "Otherwise I'll be bouncing around the court like a lead balloon."

I could see him make a mental note of that phrase for future use before grinning and saying:

"Patience, patience. You'll see."

We emptied the bowls and pushed them to one side.

"Right," said Hans patting his stomach. "Let's see how you feel after that. It's taken the edge off your appetite, yes?"

"Definitely," I nodded.

"But you could still slip down a little something extra?"

Grudgingly I admitted that I could.

"Good. We'll go on to the second course."

To my surprise, and also much to my relief, he called the waitress over, paid the bill and led me out into the Old Town again.

"The next course is taken *al fresco*," he said teasingly and guided me down one of the little cobbled alleyways until we came to a brightly-lit, covered stall standing by the side of the road. It was a sausage stall - Austria's equivalent of a hot-dog stand. Behind the counter stood an old man wearing a white apron and all around him sausages of every shape and size and colour sizzled on grills or floated in pans of boiling water.

"This is my favourite stall," said Hans. "You can get anything you want here. Do you want to choose or shall I order for you?"

"No, go on, you choose."

For himself he ordered a *Münchener* - a horrible-looking, large, fat, white, boiled sausage which reminded me of an overgrown maggot - and for me a *Burenwurst* which was a red, meaty, grilled sausage. They were both served on a small cardboard plate with a slice of rye bread and a good helping of mustard. There was also a little, two-pronged, plastic fork but, following my host's lead, I took the sausage in one hand, the bread in the other and took alternate bites from each, dipping the sausage in the mustard at regular intervals. At first I felt very self-conscious standing there in the middle of the street with my elbows on the counter eating with my hands but nobody paid us any attention. The sausage was good and, by the time I'd finished the last mouthful, I definitely wasn't hungry anymore.

"So that," said Hans wiping his hands with a serviette, "was a typical Austrian supper. Not bad, eh?"

"Not bad at all. I couldn't eat anything else if I tried."

"That's the idea you see. The soups are good here and they're not much more than a cup of coffee. It means you can sit down in comfort for a while without paying a fortune for a meal and then fill the remaining gaps with a sausage. A good supper for less than twenty-five schillings. When I was a student I used to live on soup and sausages."

"Well thanks for the experience and for buying my dinner. It was splendid."

"No, no. It wasn't splendid. Splendid means expensive." He searched his memory for the right word. "It was expedient, that's what it was."

"Yes but I'm English. According to the pupils I'm supposed to be ultra-polite. I could hardly say to my host 'thank you for an expedient dinner' now could I?"

He laughed.

"No I suppose not," he said.

When we arrived at the school the gymnasium was brightly lit and brimming with life.

"Judging by the cars it looks like most of the regulars are here already," said Hans leading me into the sports complex and through a door marked 'male staff only'.

"How many's that?" I asked as we emerged in a large, clean, modern changing room.

"About twelve as a rule, maybe fifteen on a good night. You don't want too many really or it gets too difficult to give everyone a proper game."

I'd noticed seven or eight people in the gym as we'd come past, three of them women, and there were another four men in the changing room in various states of undress. I was pleased to find Bud Ryan among them.

"Iain. Good to see ya again," he said coming over to shake my hand. "How're ya doing?"

"A good deal better than when I saw you before," I answered with a smile. "What are you doing here?"

"I always come. I've been playing volleyball Tuesday nights ever since I came to Austria. It keeps me in touch with the people at the school. By the way, I was going to give you a ring anyway. If you're still looking for a bed in town one of the Notre Dame guys is looking for a room-mate."

"Thanks very much for the thought but I've got a room in town fixed up from the beginning of next month."

Briefly I explained about finding Herbie's place.

"That sounds great," he said. "It'll certainly do your German more good than sharing with an American. Look, as soon as you move in, have a word with the landlord about coming to some arrangement with the school about reserving the room when you leave. You never know, he might be willing to let it to the English assistant every year. It wouldn't do the school any harm to pay a thousand schillings or so to keep it empty for a couple of months during the summer and it would sure as hell be one less problem for me each year. But do it now while you still remember what it felt like having nowhere to live. In a couple of months you'll have forgotten all about it."

I promised faithfully I'd do that and was led away by Hans to meet the others.

I recognised all three by sight from the staffroom but I'd never actually spoken to them. At the school they were always together since they all taught maths and shared the same absurd sense of humour. Only two days before I'd watched in amazement during morning break as they'd held a competition to see who could drink a cup of coffee with his hands behind his back. This involved lifting a half-full paper cup off the table with their teeth and slowly tilting it so that the liquid trickled down their throats. Johannes, the youngest and most lunatic of the three, a tall blond man of about twenty-eight with a big baby-face, had thrown caution to the wind and dived straight in while the other two hung back. Once he'd managed to pour a third of the contents down his shirt his colleagues had quickly conceded defeat without lifting a cup. I strongly suspected, as did Johannes, that he had been set up but they strenuously denied it. It confirmed what I had always believed, that a lot of teachers are really still children themselves. The other two, Max and Mannfred, were known in the school as Max and Moritz after two Tweedledum Tweedledee German cartoon characters. They were about the same age, in their mid-thirties, and looked very much alike too with black bushy beards full-face. They gave me a warm welcome. Mannfred clapped a hand on my shoulder and said:

"Great. You've turned up at last. We were beginning to think you didn't like volleyball."

"We always like to get the assistant to come along," added Max beaming. "It's the only chance we get to talk to you. You're always surrounded by a bodyguard from the English department at school."

"Of course you always get the odd one who outstays his welcome," Johannes piped up looking slyly at Bud. Bud rose to the bait and said something short and sharp in local dialect which I presumed was obscene from the way they all fell about laughing.

"Do you know how to play?" asked Max.

"Not a clue, I'm afraid," I told him.

"It doesn't matter we'll teach you."

I quickly got changed and went with Hans to join the group in the gym. I recognized all the faces but the only person I knew well was Suzi from the English department. I presumed that, like me, she was using volleyball as a way of getting to know people at the school.

Mannfred, who seemed to be the unofficial organiser, divided us into two teams of seven, trying to balance out experienced and inexperienced players as best he could and making sure that Hans and I were on the same side.

"You might need some help from Hans as we go along," he said to me as the two teams started to sort themselves out on either side of the net. "It can be a bit confusing at first."

This turned out to be an understatement. Seven-a-side is technically too many for a game but since volleyball involves each player moving one position clockwise on each change of service, one person each time was rotated off court. All the moving round and rapid changes of service was mind-boggling for a beginner and I spent most of the evening being pushed from one position to the next by Hans who had strategically placed himself next to me. The worst bit of all for me was serving. No matter how hard I tried I just could not get it right. The ball went everywhere except over the net into the opposing court and the shouts of 'nearly' and 'good try' and 'have another go' just seemed to make it worse. It didn't matter in the slightest, of course. The standard of the players ranged from total beginners like Suzi and me to experts like Hans and Mannfred and the whole game was played in a great spirit of fun and friendly rivalry. Every time Suzi or I got a ball back over the net it was greeted with wild applause and shouts of 'well done' and nobody really seemed too bothered who won. Towards the end, I'd begun to get more of a feel for the game and started to move into the correct position without having to be prompted by Hans. Once I understood what was going on, there was a neat regular pattern to it which I liked. It was an immensely exciting sport and I thoroughly enjoyed playing despite the difficulties and I was determined to keep coming and learn to play it properly. I also liked the atmosphere and the people. There was only one problem really, just one thing which marred my enjoyment of the evening, and that was my pride.

I liked sports and had always done reasonably well at the games I'd taken seriously and I was slightly frustrated that I was getting to know these people playing a game I wasn't any good at. Childishly I would rather have liked to have made some sort of impression, not only because of my own personal pride but also because I was a foreigner, an Englishman. It was very curious but being abroad had somehow aroused a latent patriotism that I'd never really experienced before, except perhaps when I'd been living in France. On this occasion, it proved to be my undoing.

After the game had finished and the nets had been taken down a few of the men began kicking a football around the gym. Now I could play football, at least, I could play it better than I could play volleyball, and I eagerly joined in. In fact, to be honest, I showed off to an embarrassing degree, intercepting passes, dribbling round the gym shaking off tackles and placing shots hard into the corners of the makeshift goal. I had a wonderful time and began to feel quite good that I was setting the record straight. Finally, someone passed the ball slow and high just behind me several yards from the goal. I had plenty of room so I decided to play my *piece de résistance* - an overhead scissors kick. As the ball dropped, I rolled over backwards onto the hard wooden floor and hammered the ball over my head towards the goal. It was a beautiful piece of exhibitionism and it was greeted by loud applause from the other players. Unfortunately, I wasn't in any position to enjoy the accolade. My back had gone.

A few years earlier I'd injured my back playing rugby and been bedridden for several weeks. I'd recovered eventually but from that point onwards, totally without warning, my back would suddenly take offence at something I made it do and I would be temporarily crippled again. It was a totally random ailment unfortunately. I could quite happily indulge in strenuous activities for months on end without the slightest trouble and then, often for no apparent reason, my back would go and I'd be helpless. I just couldn't believe that of all times it had to happen now.

I knew immediately what I'd done of course and felt sick inside and very angry with myself. At home it would have been easy. I knew the routine. One day lying flat trying to move about as little as possible and then gentle exercises morning and evening to ease away the tightness in the muscles. But here I had problems. For a start, I had no intention of letting anybody see I was hurt if I could help it. After all I didn't want anyone saying the English assistant couldn't handle a gentle game of volleyball followed by a knockabout with a football. Secondly, I was due to go rambling in Italy the next day and there was no way I was going to miss it. Someone might insist on taking me to a doctor or, worse still, a hospital, God forbid. I had no choice but to put a brave face on it now, get out as best I could and hope for a miracle cure overnight.

In retrospect, it was sheer stupidity. I went to Italy almost every month later in the year and spent the whole Easter holiday in Rome and Florence. Missing one day trip to South Tyrol would have made no difference whatsoever to my stay in Austria. As for my colleagues, none of them, I'm sure, was the slightest bit interested in my ability as a sportsman or in my physical prowess. They would have shown nothing but sympathy and concern if they'd realized I was hurt. But living abroad does strange things to your mind sometimes, especially at the beginning and your perspective on things easily becomes warped. At the time it all seemed vitally important to me so I played the charade through to the end.

Fortunately my final kick signalled the end of the knockabout and the players began to move slowly towards the changing room. I stayed where I was on the ground, my hands behind my head, forcing a smile as if I was just having a quick rest after all the running around.

"Come on Bobby Charlton," called Hans as he was leaving the gym, "come and get changed."

"I'll be through in a second," I answered. "You go ahead."

As soon as the coast was clear I began the painful process of getting to my feet. It was agony. Every movement sent a spasm of pain through the lower half of my body and I had to force myself not to cry out or better still swear volubly. I knew from experience that the key was keeping my back as straight as possible and that the sooner I was upright the better. In the end, I gave up trying to do it gently since it was just prolonging the agony, so, gritting my teeth against the pain, I made a supreme effort and forced myself to my feet in one continuous movement.

I thought at first I was going to faint or at least be sick but the pain slowly subsided until it was merely a dull ache again. I stood there for a while concentrating on keeping my back straight and then gently, avoiding any jerky movements, I began to shuffle towards the changing rooms. Fortunately, when I finally got there, it was empty and I could hear the others laughing and shouting in the showers. I decided showering was out of the question and that I could use their absence to put my clothes on since it was going to be a lengthy, painful exercise.

By the time they started to appear, I was dressed and sitting gingerly on a bench trying hard not to move. I was surprised that nobody mentioned the fact that I'd not taken a shower because it must have looked rather strange. I only found out much later in the year from Hans that they had all put it down to inherent English modesty and shyness.

"Right," said Mannfred as everyone finished drying and dressing, "where to tonight then? The *Kristal* as usual or somewhere different for a change?"

"The *Kristal* will do won't it?" said Max. "At least they know us there and they've probably reserved a table."

There were general murmurs of agreement from the rest of the group.

"Ok then, the *Kristal* it is." Mannfred looked at me.

"You'll come won't you? We always go for a few drinks afterwards."

I was in something of a dilemma. The whole point of playing volleyball was to get to know some of the other teachers and obviously the best way of doing that was over a few drinks. If I didn't go they would probably think I was unsociable and I didn't want that. On the other hand, I was in a bad way and the most important thing was to get home and lie down. I couldn't afford to risk it.

"Tonight's a bit of a problem," I said. "I've got the bus to catch back up to Axams and then an early start in the morning for South Tyrol. I think I'd better leave it for the evening."

It sounded like a weak excuse and Mannfred was clearly disappointed. But he didn't press the point.

"You'll come next week though won't you?" he said.

I promised I would.

That journey home is something I never want to have to repeat as long as I live. Hans dropped me at the bus station on his way to the pub in town and, as soon as he and his passengers were out of sight, I hobbled onto the bus, grateful not to have to play act anymore. It was always an uneven journey but this time I felt every single bump as the bus wound its way up the valley to the village. I was mercilessly rocked from side to side in my seat as it took bend after bend and in the end, no matter what position I adopted, I couldn't stop the pain. When we finally reached Axams I held up the driver's progress for several minutes as I struggled to get off the bus, conscious of his impatient glare in the mirror as I hobbled to the door and gingerly eased myself down the steps. But all that was the easy part, a mere taster of the real purgatory to come - the long trek up the stony tracks to the flat on the hill.

I was convinced after just a few yards that I was never going to make it and the conviction stayed with me throughout the climb. Walking uphill put a permanent strain on my back and each step caused me pain. Every so often, my foot would slip on a stone and the red-hot needles in my lower spine would stop me in my tracks. The nearer I got to the flat, the more often I was stopping, trying desperately to pull myself together enough to go on, cursing my stupidity earlier in the evening. I was uncomfortably aware, too, that the terrain in South Tyrol was likely to be a good deal rougher than these tracks and roads. It was dark and it was cold and I was fed up and miserable. I was also just a little frightened because I wasn't sure just how much longer I could keep going. But I pushed on desperately, hearing only the sound of my own footsteps scrunching on the mud and the stones. I started to count them, 1, 2, 3, 4, trying to keep my mind off the pain. It didn't help much and I'd almost decided to give up and die of exposure when, to my relief, I saw the lights of the houses on the hill. With one last effort, spurred by the knowledge that I was nearly there, I managed to cover the remaining stretch of hillside and reach the flat.

By the time I'd climbed all the stairs and let myself into the bedroom at the top, I was a wreck, completely exhausted by the effort and I just dragged off my clothes and lay down gently on the bed to sleep, hoping desperately that somehow everything would be alright in the morning.

Chapter Ten

I had a disturbed night, plagued by a nightmare in which I was endlessly struggling up a treacherous mountainside with lead weights tied to my feet and the assembled volleyball club watching my efforts, cackling maliciously and taunting me for my weakness. I eventually woke at six o'clock in a cold sweat, Viktor's voice slowly receding in my head saying: "I told you so. I told you so."

I lay there for a while, my heart racing, breathing deeply trying to shake off the effects of the dream. I wasn't due to meet Viktor for almost an hour and a half which gave me plenty of time to assess my condition and decide what I was going to do. My back didn't hurt at all, but as I was lying flat that didn't prove much. For ten minutes I lay there motionless, afraid of what I might find if I did move, but eventually I knew I had to find out one way or the other.

Tentatively I slid my legs over to the edge of the bed and tried to sit up. It wasn't easy but at the third attempt I managed to do it and perched there precariously trying to keep my back as straight as possible. The agonizing pain of the night before had dulled but it had been replaced by a stiffness that made movement almost as difficult. After a few moments rest, I stood up and began to take a few careful steps around the room. At first the stiffness was very restrictive and I could barely put one foot in front of the other but after a while it eased up slightly and I was left with a permanent dull ache in the small of my back. The only real pain accompanied any sharp jerky movement or sudden change of position. I knew that logically I was in no fit state to go clambering around hills in Italy but I was quite determined to go. I could walk and that would have to be enough.

After a hot bath which helped a little and dressing, which didn't, I met Viktor at the usual place on the main road. I eased myself gently into his little car and we drove down to the school where the coach was already waiting for us. A crowd of excited children were milling around the coach, jostling for position and waiting eagerly for permission to board, no doubt, just like English children, ready to fight for the back seat. I always felt like a visiting celebrity on occasions like this because, whenever I arrived on the scene, I immediately became the centre of attention. Today was no exception and, almost before I had struggled out of the car, I was being bombarded with questions.

"Do they have coaches like this in England, Herr 'fessor?

"I bet you'd never seen a real mountain before you came here, had you sir?"

"Do you like drinking red wine?"

"Have you ever eaten spaghetti before, Herr 'fessor?"

"Does it snow in England, sir?"

Since they knew all the answers already I assumed they just liked to talk to me and hear me speak German. They shared Viktor's pleasure in listening to me painfully constructing sentences in my own peculiar brand of German and would stand absolutely silent, shushing anyone who dared move, straining to interpret what I was saying. As I finished each stumbling sentence, I almost expected a round of applause. It was like giving a concert - "I shall now conjugate the verb 'to be' in 'A' minor."

The performance continued in the coach. Viktor had carefully sat me down next to him at the front so that he could give me a running commentary but each time he settled into a discourse on some point of interest we were interrupted by a boy or a pair of girls - the girls always hunted in pairs - offering me a sandwich or a biscuit or a cake or a drink of coke or anything which they assumed I would never have come across in darkest England. They seemed to view it as some kind of backward third-world country cut off from the mainstream of European civilisation. Whenever I asked them about British eating habits I was always told we ate eggs and bacon for breakfast, roast beef for lunch and took tea and cucumber sandwiches in the afternoon. Every day. It took quite a lot to persuade them that even the English might want to vary this regime occasionally.

It's always nice to be made a fuss of and I enjoyed the interruptions immensely. In just a few weeks I'd grown to love the Austrian children. The assistant in a school holds a very special position in the eyes of the pupils. On the one hand, he's a real live example of the kind of people they spend every English lesson reading about, a kind of yardstick against which they can measure the accuracy of what they've been taught. On the other he's a teacher with none of the teacher's responsibilities. He doesn't give exams or marks, write notes to their parents or set them homework. His lessons are a break from the normal dull routine, even if they're not wonderfully entertaining in themselves, and classes tend to look forward to them. And since the pupils gave me so much pleasure when they responded in class, I tried to respond to them as much as possible outside. At first Viktor was annoyed at the interruptions, more on my behalf than his own but, once he saw that I quite enjoyed the attentions lavished upon me, he let them play themselves out. Eventually, the supply of food and questions seemed to run out or, perhaps, the novelty wore off, and we were left in peace.

It took only half-an-hour to cross the low flat Brenner pass through the Alps and reach the border with Italy. Being pitifully ignorant about geography I was surprised at how near it was to Innsbruck. We were waved straight through the Austrian customs but at the Italian border we were forced to stop and a small, fat immigration officer boarded the coach.

"This lot all Austrian, then?" he said to me, the nearest adult. I wasn't quite sure how to respond to this so Viktor quickly took over.

"They are, he isn't."

"What's he then?" asked the officer.

"I'm English," I said, deciding it was time to speak for myself.

"You see," said the officer with a broad grin, "picked out the villain first time. That's why I'm an immigration officer. Got the nose for it. I don't suppose you've got a passport by any chance. You're probably on my wanted list."

Obediently, I began to reach in my pocket but he held up his hand and said with a smile:

"That's alright, I believe you. Have a good time."

He left the coach and waved us through.

"Are all the border officials like that?" I asked Viktor.

"Most of them. Historically this bit of Italy is part of Austria and deep down inside the people are still Austrians. They're not going to make it difficult for us to come in and out - their relatives do it all the time. Since you're with us, he granted you the status of honorary

Austrian. Anyway," he grinned mischievously, "the kids would probably have lynched him if he'd given you any trouble."

Just across the border, on the outskirts of Brenner itself, there were rows and rows of market stalls selling leather goods, wines and spirits.

"That's where most Tyroleans do their shopping," explained Viktor. "They pop over the border, buy shoes, bags and as much wine and spirits as they're allowed and drive back. Even allowing for the cost of petrol, they save a fair amount compared with the prices in Austria."

I would have quite liked to stop and have a look around but that wasn't why we were there unfortunately. The coach pushed on through the town and out into the countryside beyond. The road wound along through the valley with the mountains rising either side of us clothed in their coats of pine trees. It was too early for skiing and most of the lifts were still and silent but now and again I caught a glimpse between the peaks of a chair rocking gently in the mountain breezes, taking early sightseers up 3,000 metres to the top of the *Cima-Bianca* over in the East. The landscape was extraordinarily beautiful and peaceful and I was happy to sit watching peaks, pinewoods, small lakes and the occasional castle passing by on either side. I began to wish we were spending the whole day touring in the coach. I was quite comfortable now and had no desire whatsoever to get up and start walking about but, after an hour or so, my peace was disturbed and we made our first stop of the day.

"This is Brixen," said Viktor. "We'll stop here for a while first just to get settled before the walk."

"I thought the sign said it was Bressanone," I pointed out, confused.

"That's what the Italians call it," he answered with a wry smile. "But what do they know?"

We drew into the centre of the town and the coach parked. Viktor stood up and addressed the pupils.

"Right, we're going to stop here for forty minutes only and I want you back on the coach by ten-thirty, After that the coach will drop us in the hills and we can have a good walk before lunch. I suggest you all go to the toilet, have a drink if you want one or look around the shops.

We may get a chance to visit Meran or Bolzen later but if there is anything particular you want to bring back buy it here just in case. OK, off you go and don't be late back."

Almost before he'd finished there was mad rush for the door and in seconds the coach was empty save for Viktor, his two colleagues and me.

"Right let's all go and have a drink," suggested Viktor.

"Actually, if you don't mind, I'd rather like to have a look around the town," I told him. I felt it was time to give my back some exercise before the main event.

"Of course. How foolish of me. I forgot for a moment that you'd not been here before. I'll come with you if you like and show you the sights."

"No, that's OK. I'll just take a quick walk round just so I can say I've been here. You go and have drink."

"Well, if you're quite sure, we'll see you back here later."

I can't honestly say I was much impressed by Brixen. I have a vague recollection of a rather nice cathedral and some cloisters adjoining it leading to a museum but apart from that nothing else struck me particularly. Not that I was in the ideal mood for sightseeing. My back had stiffened up during the coach ride and I was moving awkwardly again. I was getting very worried about the next stage in the day's entertainment. Although I could walk unaided, the slightest jolt caused me some pain and that was on nice even pavements. Two or three hours of rambling over rough hillsides was going to do me no good at all. I spent most of my time in the town looking round the shops as usual. A good many things were cheaper than in Innsbruck and since my finances were at a low ebb I bought some coffee, which was exorbitantly expensive in Austria. None of the souvenirs tempted me at all and after forty minutes I wandered back to the coach.

The masses reassembled and once they'd been counted six or seven times by an already irritated Viktor the coach set off into the hills.

"Right," said Viktor with a heavy sigh as he sat back down, "this is the plan. The coach is going to take us up to the start of one of the recognised walks, there are quite a few marked out round here, then he'll drive back down into the village at the bottom of the route and wait for us. We walk down in our own time, have a leisurely lunch in the village and then, depending on the time, go on somewhere else. How does that sound?"

It sounded wonderful if you were fit.

The coach ploughed on away from the town, out past the main Brenner road and began to climb a steep mountain road leading up one side of the valley. Soon, on either side of the road there was nothing but pine forests as far as the eye could see, criss-crossed here and there with tracks covered in cones and needles. Higher and higher we went, catching the occasional glimpse back down into the valley through the gaps in the pines as the road wound round and round and doubled back on itself. Finally, a large clearing appeared just ahead on the left-hand side of the road with a wooden sign announcing that this was the entrance to walk number two. Large wooden arrows behind it pointed the way invitingly into the depths of the forest.

The coach stopped in the clearing and Viktor got to his feet again.

"Right, this is it," he said. "Now you all know the rules. You are all to stay within sight of one of the members of staff at all times. *Herr Professor* Kroll will be the front-marker and I will be the rearguard. Nobody is to walk behind me or more than 50 metres in front of Herr Kroll. Is that understood?"

"Yes, *Herr 'fessor*," the children chorused, already on their feet and dragging bags down from the racks as the doors of the coach shushed open to let us out.

It now occurred to me for the first time that I was pathetically ill-prepared for a ramble. I'd noticed already the highly professional backpacks that most of the group sported but now, as we prepared to go, they began to put on thick socks and stout walking boots. All I had was a pair of battered shoes and a carrier bag containing my coffee. I had a feeling that this was going to be a disaster.

In fact, to start with it wasn't a disaster at all. It was a glorious day for a walk and, in retrospect, I wouldn't have missed it for the world. There had obviously been a shower that morning and as we entered the forest I was hit by the cool clean scent of the pines mingled with the smell of the damp earth and grass. Droplets of water glistened on the trees, the birds sang all around us and the ground was soft and moist underfoot. It was almost unbelievably idyllic, like something out of a Disney cartoon. It was a well-trodden path, obviously popular with hill-walkers and it meandered gently down between the trees posing no great challenge even to an invalid like me. Once I'd got going and the stiffness had eased a little I found that I could walk with only minimal discomfort provided I was careful. I'd almost begun to believe that everything was going to be alright after all and that I needn't have worried unduly, when the going suddenly got tougher and we moved away from the forest and out onto a much steeper track leading down to another wooded area about a mile away. My back had already started to ache a little from the exertions on the gentle slope and the new slippery stone track soon made walking extremely painful. To make matters worse, the track was crossed at intervals by small shallow streams and, since I couldn't jump them as the others were doing, I was having to pick my way through them. Before long my feet were saturated adding considerably to my discomfort.

This proved to be the general pattern of the walk - a gentle wooded stretch followed by a much more difficult trek across country to another wooded stretch. I was having to rest as much as possible in the woods, taking advantage of the easier terrain to try and regain enough strength to cope with the next difficult bit. However, by the time we reached the last cross-country stretch, I'd become a complete automaton, totally oblivious to the wonderful countryside I was supposed to be enjoying, aware only of my cold, wet feet and the pain in my back. All I wanted to do was lie down somewhere and sleep for a week.

At last, after about two hours, a village came into sight and the track levelled off into a paved road leading to some houses. Viktor, who had been kept busy throughout the walk keeping together the children, none of whom had paid the slightest attention to his earlier instructions, came over and joined me.

"Well that was rather pleasant, wasn't it?" he said. "Now for the wine and spaghetti. I bet you're dying for something to eat after all that walking."

Just dying would have been more accurate but I managed to force a smile and say how much I'd enjoyed it.

"That's good. We'll probably have time for another one this afternoon with any luck."

I forced another sickly smile and he went back to counting the kids again.

We were booked to have lunch in the village inn and a large upstairs room had been reserved for us. Wooden tables had been pushed together in rows for the pupils and one smaller table had been left at one end of the room for the adults. I took my place at this table and a heaped plate of steaming spaghetti topped with a rich meat and tomato sauce was placed in front of me. Viktor called for a jug of red wine and four glasses and soon, warmed by the food and the alcohol, I began to recover from the exertions of the last few hours. By the end of the meal, under the influence of several glasses of red wine, I was beginning to feel a bit more human again. The ache in my back had receded behind a light alcoholic daze and I was almost ready to have another crack at the hills. Luckily for me, however, Viktor decided it was too late to do any more walking.

"I think we've just got time to have a look around Meran before we head back," he said collecting up our money and paying the bill. "You'll like it. If nothing else it's a good deal more impressive than Brixen."

He was right. I did like it and went back several times during my stay in Austria. I was particularly taken by the old main street, the dark narrow Via de Portici, containing not only most of the principal tourist attractions of Meran, or Merano as the Italians called it, but also, beneath its low arcades, some excellent shops. Being something of a Philistine, and having an unnatural attraction to anywhere where I could spend money, I was tempted to spend the time looking around the shops but Viktor had obviously decided that I would benefit from a little education.

"Come on," he said, "you can't possibly leave here without visiting the *Castello Principesco*. It was built by Archduke Sigismund in the fifteenth century."

I tried to force my features into a look which said that my life would be incomplete without seeing something built by Archduke Sigismund in the Fifteenth Century and followed him.

Once inside he led me straight to a wall where the arms of Scotland were prominently displayed next to those of Austria.

"You see," he announced proudly, "there's a part of your history here too. Archduke Sigismund married Eleanor, the daughter of your James I. Our two countries were tied together almost five hundred years ago."

I couldn't possibly resist this call on my patriotism so I followed him obediently around the rest of the building, amazed at his fund of historical knowledge and unusual little anecdotes. He then took me to down to the Gothic church at the end of the road and showed me the strange battlement-like facade and the two altarpieces inside by Martin Knoller. It was like sightseeing with a walking, talking Michelin guide book. Finally, after an hour's intensive research, he decided I'd had enough culture for one day and let me wander aimlessly through the arcades and then down to the banks of the river where the very expensive, more fashionable shops stood. Neither of us bought anything but we enjoyed it all the same and with Viktor's help I picked up lots of good new vocabulary, including such wonderfully useful words as 'nail-clipper' and 'electric shaver'.

"I shall wait with baited breath for you to use some of that new vocabulary at school in conversation," said Viktor as we walked back to the coach. "I can just imagine the look on Frau Grindl's face when you ask her for a loan of her nail-clipper."

"Or, even better, her electric shaver," I suggested.

Viktor laughed and went off to find out how many of his precious charges were still missing.

The wine at lunch had made me very drowsy and I slept most of the way back to Innsbruck. By the time we arrived home I was feeling distinctly ill again. As the wine wore off the pain in my back returned with a vengeance and I now had a raging headache to go with it. But unfortunately the day wasn't over just yet. I was dependent on Viktor for a lift home and he of course still had his responsibilities as a teacher. Once we were off the coach, I had to stand around in the cold for what seemed like a lifetime while Viktor sorted out the excited, chattering children and made sure they were all there and in a fit state to go home. Only then could he drive me back to Axams, thankfully taking me right to the door of the flat. Out of politeness, I invited him in for a coffee but fortunately he refused and gratefully I went straight to bed.

The next morning I rang Reiner at eight o'clock and told him the whole story, sure that he would understand. He found the whole episode highly entertaining and told me to skip the day's lessons and come in again on Monday. I was still worried about the others though, determined that, having played the charade through this far, they shouldn't find out now.

"Don't worry," he said when I mentioned my concern, "I won't breathe a dickybird. Your terrible secret is safe with me."

"But what will you tell them?"

He thought for a moment and then started to laugh.

"That's easy enough. I'll tell them you've got sausage poisoning."

He was still laughing when I put the phone down and went back to bed.

Chapter Eleven

"You realize it's almost the beginning of November and we haven't so much as clapped eyes on the other French assistant," said Mike dolefully one lunchtime as we sat over our now habitual coffee and cake.

"Well you're the one who works in the same school as Maurice," I told him, "tell him to get her out one evening."

"Fat chance. You know as well as I do that the *entente* is far from *cordiale* at the moment."

I did indeed know. Relations with Maurice had improved slightly after the initial setback only to sink to an all-time low when Mike, in a fit of pique in response to the suggestion that Shakespeare had written only one good play, had systematically demolished French culture for the last 600 years. Maurice now avoided us at lunchtimes and confined himself to strictly formal greetings at school.

"Well the choice is yours," I said, "either you apologise or remain forever in ignorance of whether Mlle X has good legs or not."

Mike was thoughtful for a moment.

"I suppose you're right, damn it," he said, "I'll have to make the sacrifice and crawl to him. Mind you, so will you. I can't just say 'sorry Maurice, now what's the French girl's number'. It would be too obvious. We are going to have to start meeting him socially on a regular basis and drag it out of him gradually."

"Alright then. Apologise to him tomorrow and ask him out to dinner with us on Saturday."

"OK. I'll do that. No, hang on, aren't we taking part in this AFS nonsense on Saturday?"

"Yes. But that shouldn't drag on into the evening. And even if it does look like going on, we've got a good excuse for disappearing."

AFS was the Association for Foreign Students in Innsbruck and they had organised a trip up into the mountains on Saturday. Mike and I weren't exactly desperate to take part. AFS catered primarily for American and English students in the town and we weren't particularly keen on meeting either. Unfortunately, Mike had been formally invited through his landlady by the secretary at the Embassy who had helped him find his room and he'd felt it would be churlish to refuse. He'd also decided it would be churlish to deprive me of such a wonderful experience and had volunteered my name as well. I was totally underwhelmed by this generosity and at first I'd refused point blank even to consider it but after much wheedling and cajoling and calls on my loyalty I'd agreed, much against my better judgement, to accompany him. Neither of us was particularly looking forward to Saturday.

The next day, however, things looked up considerably. When I met Mike at lunchtime, prior to going off to eat in the *Mensa* he was remarkably cheerful.

"Hey, guess what," he said.

"No, don't tell me. You've volunteered me for an Outward Bound weekend in Tibet with AFS, right?"

"No, better than that. I saw Maurice this morning and grovelled to him. All our problems are solved. When I asked him if he'd like to meet us on Saturday for dinner he said he was already meeting the other French assistant. So I smoothly suggested we all meet together in the *Goldene Löwe* at seven-thirty and he agreed. We're in! Apparently she's been asking to meet us anyway. Her name's Chantal."

This was great news. Our social life so far had not exactly been exciting. We'd been in Austria over a month and neither of us had much more than a nodding acquaintance with any of the local people. I was luckier than Mike in that I still saw Hans quite often outside school but I suspected that this would tail off once I moved out of his flat. And anyway our meetings were confined to the occasional drink together during the week. Hans had his own social life at weekends. Every Saturday so far had seen Mike and I on our own eating and drinking in the *Goldene Löwe*. This was alright as far as it went but it wasn't really getting us anywhere. For a start, we knew it wouldn't be long before we started to get on each other's nerves and, more importantly, we were still speaking English together all the time since there was nobody there to make us speak German. We'd tried unsuccessfully several times to give Jane and Gerhardt the thank-you dinner we'd promised them but they seemed to be caught up in an almost continuous whirl of social engagements which just made our own situation seem that much worse.

We were both going through a bad patch generally at the time. We had been in Innsbruck a month and were both showing all the traditional symptoms of cultural shock. We had been cheated a couple of times in shops since all foreigners were seen as fair game and this had prompted an 'I hate Austrians' phase. In addition we were both convinced that our German hadn't improved at all even though we spoke it at school every day. To cap it all neither of us had much money left.

In reality, neither Mike nor myself had any real reason to feel dissatisfied with our lot. We had both been accepted easily into our respective schools, got on well with our new colleagues and enjoyed the teaching we did. I had very quickly got through the probationary period, having demonstrated no outrageous political leanings or expressed any heretical religious views, and in all but Reiner's classes, I was given free rein to do what I liked. Reiner for some reason didn't seem at all willing to let me teach his classes but I hadn't bothered to press the point. I was quite happy to sit and listen to his tireless stream of outrageous jokes and insults which went largely uncomprehended by his pupils. Mike and I both took the work seriously and this was respected by our supervisors. It was only outside work that life in Austria so far had not lived up to expectations.

Friday, the day before the AFS outing, was when I'd arranged to move out of Axams into Herbie's place and the week passed all too quickly in the now familiar routine of teaching. I was rather apprehensive about moving into the town. I'd got used to having the large luxurious flat all to myself and it was going to be difficult adapting to sharing bathrooms and kitchens with people again. I'd gone round the village in the morning and said my goodbyes to the shopkeepers, particularly the lady in the grocery store, and that had made me rather sad. Although I'd said I'd come back up and see them from time to time I knew that I probably wouldn't go back often, if at all. Once I'd settled into Innsbruck, Axams would soon just become a pleasant memory.

I found the business of packing my belongings and tidying the flat even more depressing and by the time Hans arrived to drive me down to Herbie's I was feeling very sorry for myself. The last month had involved so many upheavals and changes that I just couldn't face another one. I was fed with walking into the unknown at weekly intervals, adapting like a chameleon to constantly changing circumstances. I toyed briefly with the idea of asking Hans if I could stay in Axams and pay him a realistic rent for the flat but it wasn't really a serious or a sensible proposition. For a start, he was selling the place and I couldn't possibly pay him enough to make renting it worthwhile and, more importantly, I needed the experience of living among native speakers or I'd never learn to speak German properly. There was also the problem of having a social life regulated by the last bus. At the moment, it didn't matter too much since I didn't have much of a social life but if things worked out with Chantal and Maurice it would be critical. I knew I'd be alright once I'd settled in, it was just the initial change that was difficult.

On the way into town Hans stopped off at his bank and returned with a thousand schillings.

"Here you are," he said handing me the money, "your first month's rent. They'll want it in advance."

"Shouldn't I be giving you rent?" I asked him, gratefully pocketing the notes, "not the other way around."

"Oh, we'll worry about all that when you get paid. It shouldn't be long now."

"Thanks Hans. I'll pay you back immediately I get the money.

He waved away the thanks.

"It's alright. No problem. Anyway how do you feel about moving into town at last?"

"Mixed feelings. I liked it up there, you know, even though I never really got into the life of the place." I'd never summoned up enough courage to go for that drink. "It's got a quiet charm all of its own."

"I liked it too," he said with a hint of sadness. "I miss it sometimes."

"Well you could move back one day if you didn't sell."

He shrugged his shoulders.

"No choice. I have to sell it to pay off my ex-wife. She's already breathing down my neck. Anyway the sale's too far gone to be stopped. I'll just have to buy another place in the mountains somewhere when I can afford it again."

"I'd like to do that too, one day."

Hans smiled.

"Is that before or after you emigrate to Australia, teach English in Japan and join the Foreign Office?"

These were some of the many options for my future we'd explored in our late night drinking sessions.

"Maybe instead," I answered, "who knows?"

"Well, anyway, you'd better wait until you've seen a village under several feet of snow, totally cut off from the outside before you make that decision. It's a different world."

"Don't worry. I've got time to see dozens of winters before I'll be able to afford it. I shan't be rushing into anything.

"Good," he said, laughing.

Before long we drew up outside the house in Kaiser-Franz-Josef-Strasse. It was the first time I'd been back there since accepting the room and somehow the house itself and the area around it looked rather less inviting than they had in my desperate need to find somewhere to live. Hans, however, was encouraging.

"This is a nice area," he said as we got out of the car. "One of the more select suburbs of Innsbruck. You've done alright."

Together we walked up to the front door and I rang the appropriate bell. Unexpectedly a female voice answered.

"Who is it," she asked.

"My name's Iain Moss," I answered, my face almost touching the intercom. "I'm moving in today."

"Oh yes. Herbie said you were coming. Hang on, I'll let you in."

The door buzzed and we pushed our way into the hallway.

In the entrance to the flat stood a short, pretty, dark-haired girl in her late twenties. In her arms she held a baby wrapped tightly in a white shawl. She smiled as we approached.

"Hi," she said, "I'm Ingrid and this is Julia. We're going to be your neighbours. Come on in."

She closed the door behind us and called out.

"Herbie. Der Iain ist hier."

From his study at the end of the corridor Herbie appeared smiling broadly.

"Hi there. Good to see you again. All ready to move in?"

"Just about. This is Hans, one of my colleagues from school. I've been living with him up to now."

Hans and Herbie shook hands. It soon became clear that Hans had appointed himself my guardian and protector and, before we proceeded to the formalities, he questioned Herbie at length about the whole setup. He asked many of the important questions that I'd forgotten such as the possibility of the rent being increased and the period of notice I could expect if they wanted me to leave. Herbie patiently answered the questions, clearly aware of Hans' concern for my well-being, until Hans seemed satisfied, if grudgingly, that I wasn't moving into a den of thieves.

The formalities themselves were virtually non-existent. Herbie showed me the room again to make sure I didn't want to change my mind, handed me the keys and gave me a pile of bank paying-in slips made out to his parents account.

"You just take one of these along to any branch of the Landesbank once a month and hand it over with your rent. Nothing to it. Apart from that we'll talk about the electricity bills as and when they arrive."

That was it. I was in.

Herbie decided to give me a chance to settle in before introducing me to everyone so Hans and I went to unload my luggage from the car. It only needed one trip and my worldly goods were soon heaped in a pile in the middle of the room. Just like the first day in the flat, Hans was reluctant to leave me on my own, convinced there was something else he ought to be doing for me, but eventually he realised that there really was nothing and allowed me to walk him to his car.

"Now you remember, I'm always ready to help if you get any problems," he said, opening the car door. "I think you'll be OK here, they seem nice enough, but if there's any trouble you let me know. Some people think they can do what they like to you if you're a foreigner but if anyone tries it on you they'll have to answer to me."

I looked at Hans, six foot three and fifteen stone of solid muscle, and decided that it was highly unlikely that anyone would stay around long enough to answer to him.

"Don't worry Hans. I'll be fine here. They're really alright."

He got into the car and switched on the ignition.

"Right then," he said," I'll see you at school on Monday. Take care of yourself."

"Thanks for everything. I couldn't have got by without you."

He again waved away the thanks and drove off.

It didn't take me long to find out that my new home lacked a few of the more obvious home comforts. After I'd unpacked and put everything away in the ample cupboard space provided I took a closer look at the room. It was big certainly and well-furnished and the large bay-window looking out onto the street let in plenty of light. But there was no bedside lamp or table and no bedclothes, not one solitary sheet or blanket. I would have no alternative but to buy a lamp and set up an improvised bedside cabinet because I couldn't do without either. I was a chronic insomniac and had read myself to sleep ever since I could remember. My last conscious act every night was to reach out and switch off the lamp as I dropped off. If I had to get out of bed to switch off the main light I might never get to sleep. As for bedclothes, I would have to borrow what I could and buy anything else that I needed. In fact, I'd better talk to Herbie about it straight away. It was now winter in Innsbruck and I had no desire to spend even one night without warm covers, especially with no supply of coal for the oven.

I went and knocked at the door of Herbie's study.

"Hi there," he said, opening the door, "how are you settling in?"

"I've got a bit of a problem. I don't have any bedclothes."

Herbie was thoughtful for a moment or two.

"There used to be some things in there, I'm sure, before Michelle moved in. She had her own stuff so she didn't want them. I wonder what she did with them. Look, let's go and see Ingrid. She might know."

We walked back down the corridor and Herbie knocked on the door next to mine.

"Come on in," Ingrid called.

On a small sofa in a room about half the size of mine Ingrid was changing the baby. On the right, there was an open door leading into a tiny bedroom totally filled by a double bed. To the left, there was a

117

door in the wall, securely bolted, corresponding to the door I'd noticed in my room. These had obviously been interconnecting rooms at one time and that was another problem I hadn't foreseen. I could hear my own radio quite clearly through the door, even though it was only playing softly and I began to worry about my privacy a little.

"Ingrid," said Herbie, "do you happen to know what Michelle did with the bedclothes that were in the room when she moved in? We can't find them."

"Yes I do," replied Ingrid, applying the last safety pin to the nappy and kissing the baby on the forehead. "We threw them away. And lucky for you that we did. If your mother had seen them, she would have hit the roof."

"Oh God," said Herbie crestfallen, "were they bad?"

"They were a mess, Herbie, dirty and full of holes. The quilt was leaking feathers and the pillow had so many sharp ends sticking out of it you could have used it to shave."

"Oh God," said Herbie again. "I should have checked. What are we going to do for Iain?"

Ingrid was thoughtful for a moment, considering the problem.

"Well", she said, "you must phone your mother and tell her you threw out the old covers before Michelle moved in. Michelle didn't need them since she had her own but Iain does and could she supply some new ones. In the meantime I can lend him a sheet, a pillow, a sleeping-bag and a couple of blankets as a temporary measure."

Herbie cheered up immediately and threw his arms around Ingrid.

"You're marvellous," he said. "What on earth would I do without you?"

"I sometimes wonder," she replied. "Now you better get back to your studies. You've got exams next week."

"Neurology," he said to me. "It's a hard life being a medical student and a landlord. I'll see you later."

He went back to his study and Ingrid and I got down to the business of finding me something to sleep on.

Half-an-hour later I was back in my room, my bed made up to my satisfaction, a chair serving as a temporary bedside table. I had also found a candle welded to an old saucer and I'd placed this by the bed in the vain hope that it would cast enough light to read by. It was by now late in the afternoon and I had to go out and by some groceries before the shops closed. Ingrid had invited me to have dinner with herself and Rolf but I still hadn't learned and I assumed, as with Bud, that she was just being polite so I'd feigned a dinner engagement that evening. It was my loss because I discovered later that Ingrid was a superb cook and it would have helped tide me over my temporary financial difficulties. It also made things awkward now because I would have to go out that evening. I decided to buy some bread and cheese and things that I could safely keep in my room, go out to the cinema, and then eat secretly in my room when I came back. I didn't want to hurt Ingrid's feelings.

When I got back later that night the house was quiet and there were no lights to be seen. Everyone was in bed. I had to get up early the next morning so I had a quick supper and then followed their example. The sleeping bag was uncomfortable and constricting after the quilt I'd got used to, the bed was hard and the candle was worse than useless for reading by. The baby had begun to cry next door and I could hear a man's voice, Rolf's presumably, claiming loudly that it wasn't his turn. The baby cried louder and more urgently and voices raised in argument. I blew out the candle, covered my head with a pillow to blot out the noise and lay there in the dark feeling sorry for myself and wishing I was back in Axams.

Chapter Twelve

A restless, miserable, depressing night finally dissolved into a beautiful, sunny, crisp winter's day. With some relief, I set off early to meet Mike at our normal place in the Old Town. Mike was already there pacing up and down not looking particularly happy.

"Hi Mike. All set?"

"What on earth are we doing here," he answered mournfully.

"Philosophers have spent years trying to fathom that one," I said brightly.

He gave me a withering glance. He clearly wasn't in the mood for sarcasm this morning.

"You know what I mean. This AFS thing. Do you really want to go hiking round some mountain with a gang of people we don't know? I mean it's not even as if we're dressed for it."

Like me, Mike was wearing his overcoat and everyday shoes.

"Well you got us into this mess," I pointed out. "I never wanted to go. Anyway it's a bit late to back out now. We'll just have to grin and bear it."

"You know I couldn't say no. She was trying to help and I didn't want to hurt her feelings. I mean she got me my room and......."

I stopped him before he got carried away.

"OK, OK. I'm not really holding it against you. Well not much anyway. Come on let's just go and get it over with."

AFS headquarters was in a small side street between Maria-Theresien-Strasse and the river and it didn't take us long to get there, or at least in sight of it, for as we rounded the corner we saw down the road ahead of us a group of about a dozen people milling around on the pavement. They were all kitted out in full hiking gear with warm windcheaters, stout boots, woollen socks over thick outdoor trousers and backpacks. As one man Mike and I stopped in our tracks and disappeared back round the corner.

"Bloody hell," said Mike, "they look as if they're on their way to the North Pole."

"And here's us with no Bovril and no Kendall mint cake," I

replied. I was beginning to enjoy this immensely. It was all turning into a glorious joke as far as I was concerned. I wasn't exactly a keen hiker but I wasn't averse to the exercise either. I liked sport even if I wasn't particularly fit and provided my back wasn't going through one of its periodic bouts of non-cooperation, I could easily cope with a mountain hike, boots or no boots. It certainly couldn't be more difficult than South Tyrol had been. Mike, on the other hand, hated sports and had a positive aversion to physical exercise of any kind. A real hike, as opposed to a gentle ramble, was enough to give him a heart attack. His face was a picture of sheer disbelief and misery. Surreptitiously he peered round the corner again, presumably in the hope that his first look had been an hallucination.

"What are we going to do?" he asked. "They'll think we're mad dressed like this."

"If we keep standing here peering round the corner the rest of the world is going to think we're mad and have us arrested. We'll just have to go along and pretend the English always dress like this for mountaineering. You can tell them that that's the actual Marks and Spencer overcoat worn by Sir Edmund Hilary when he conquered Everest."

Mike gave me another withering look.

"You're not taking this seriously, are you?"

"Well let's face it," I said, "this is a bloody silly situation. Two grown men hanging around on a street corner trying to decide whether to go for a walk or not."

"Alright then, Mr. Mature Adult, what do we do?"

"We go as we are. Come on."

"Er, no, hang about."

For ten minutes we stood there debating the point with Mike disappearing at intervals to look round the corner. I had no desire at all to go on this trip any more than Mike but I was enjoying getting my own back for being roped into it against my will. I knew full well that if we delayed long enough the decision would make itself. Sure enough a few moments later a minibus drew up beside the assembled hikers.

"If we're going, it has to be now," I told him.

Neither of us made a move until the minibus was safely out of sight.

"Oh dear," I said laughing, "we missed it."

"My God," said Mike, looking much relieved, "the thought of nearly having to do all that exercise has given me an appetite. Let's go and get some breakfast."

We went as always to the little coffee house near the University. Unlike lunchtimes, it was almost empty and it made a pleasant change not to have to fight for a table or eat under the watchful glare of someone waiting to take your place. We ordered fresh baked rolls and croissants with jam and a pot of rich breakfast coffee and sat back ready to start the day in style.

"What are you going to tell your landlady if she asks why you didn't turn up?" I asked Mike.

"The truth of course," he replied. "You turned up late having overslept and when we arrived at the AFS the minibus was just disappearing round the corner. Unfortunate but unavoidable."

"That's the truth as you see it, is it?"

"Well it's near enough. It could have been true."

"If I'd been late."

"If you'd been late, yes."

"And if we hadn't spent several hours hiding round the corner."

"Exactly. Oh look here comes breakfast."

After we'd made deep inroads into the first basket of rolls and croissants, conversation turned to the less controversial topic of how we were going to spend the rest of the day.

"Since I'm now resident here I want to do something special to mark the occasion. Any ideas?"

"Well," said Mike after a few moments thought, "just past where I live, at the end of the tram line, there's a castle, Schloss Ambras. I rather fancy having a look round it. There's a museum of weapons and armour, paintings and antique furniture and things and the grounds are supposed to be really beautiful. My landlady keeps saying I should go and visit it."

"You could tell her I turned up late and when we got there it was gone."

"Alright, alright. I apologise for dragging you there in the first place and for using you as the scapegoat to my landlady. Now can we please forget it?"

"Apology accepted."

"Good. What about Schloss Ambras?"

I shrugged.

"It's as good a plan as any. It's about time we saw some of the sights. I mean I'd hate to spend a year here and then go home and find I'd missed something important."

"Well I don't know that it's particularly important. It's hardly the first place that springs to mind when someone mentions Innsbruck. It just looks like it might be an interesting place to spend an afternoon, that's all."

"I'm game. Let's go."

"Great. We can have a leisurely breakfast then take a long slow walk through town over to my place." He took another roll and broke it expertly in half before reaching for the butter and jam. "Have you decided what you're going to buy yet?"

"Not really," I answered. "I change my mind every day. That's part of the fun."

Over the last two weeks, with our money dwindling away to nothing, Mike and I had kept our spirits up by promising ourselves a present as soon as the first paycheque arrived. According to the rules of the game, it had to be something totally extravagant, even frivolous, that we wouldn't otherwise have bought, and we had hours of fun, both together and on our own, wandering around the shops looking for ideas.

"I've got it narrowed down to two at the moment," I continued, "although I'll probably change my mind again. It's either going to be one of those ornaments out of mountain crystal, you know, the ones that shine different colours when the light catches them, or a really good cigarette lighter."

Mike stopped eating and looked at me sceptically.

"But you don't smoke."

"Yes I do," I answered defensively. "I smoke little cigars."

"Not very often though."

"I do. A couple a week anyway."

123

"Yes but...."

He suddenly checked himself and raised his hand.

"Sorry. Out of order. We agreed not to question each other's choice."

"Ok I forgive you. What about you?"

"Well since breakfast is my favourite meal of the day, I've decided I'd like some kind of gadget to make life easier in the morning."

"What like a toast-making alarm and egg-boiler?"

"Don't be silly. I did consider a Teasmade though and an electric toaster but they seemed a bit too extravagant. I'll just have to keep working on it."

He looked thoughtfully at the last remaining roll and then decided he'd had enough."

"Actually, there are some really good shops over my way," he continued, finishing his coffee and wiping the flakes of croissant off his jumper, "ones you haven't seen before. We could go over there and have a good look round, have our packed lunches in the castle grounds and then spend the afternoon going round the castle itself. How about it?"

This was my warped idea of a perfect day.

Schloss Ambras was about twenty minutes walk away from Mike's place and we followed the tram lines down towards the terminus until we could see the castle perched on the hill overlooking the town and then climbed up the hill into the castle grounds. It looked like an ideal place to spend a bright sunny winter's afternoon. The grounds seemed to stretch for miles - the uneven park-like area in front of the castle giving way to woods in the distance.

"What shall we do first then?" asked Mike as we approached the entrance archway. "Look inside or take a walk?"

"Let's look inside. They might close early on a Saturday afternoon."

We walked inside and Mike gave a groan of disappointment.

"Damn," he said, "it looks like they closed earlier than we

thought - like three months ago."

He indicated a large notice announcing that the museum and public galleries were undergoing renovations and would be closed to the public until January. They were obviously taking advantage of the off-season to recuperate from the onslaught of tourists.

"That's a pity," I said. "I suppose we'll just have to make do with a picnic in the grounds."

"I've got a better idea," said Mike, "why don't we go up into the mountains?"

I looked at him in disbelief.

"You're joking, I take it."

"No, I'm serious."

"What, after all that fuss this morning, you have the gall to suggest we go for a ramble in the mountains?"

"Not a ramble like the Sherpas would have gone for. Not the kind you need ropes, crampons and a lobotomy for. I mean a ramble in the old-fashioned English sense. A gentle walk in the fresh air through breathtaking countryside with places every 100 yards where you can drink tea and eat cakes. That kind of ramble."

"And where do we find this alpine equivalent of Hampstead Heath?"

He smiled.

"Right next door to where you live," he said, smugly.

Two tram rides later we arrived at the circular building which served as the valley station of the *Hungerburg* funicular railway, about 200 yards from my new lodgings. We bought two tickets and went through to wait for the curious contraption which was slowly making its way towards us down the steep mountain railway line. It looked more like a lop-sided, scrunched-up, red concertina than a train. Since it spent its life being dragged up and down the mountainside by a system of cogs and cables set between the rails, always lying against the incline, it was designed accordingly.

Gently, it pulled into the covered waiting area and came to rest between the two platforms. Even though it was empty, that was no excuse for deviating from standard procedure and the doors furthest away from us were opened first to allow descending passengers off before ascending passengers crammed their way in from the other side. Our doors opened and Mike and I did the best we could to look like bustling crowds as we stepped in and sat down on a wooden bench looking back down the valley. A few moments later the doors hissed shut automatically, a klaxon blared out, synchronised presumably with a klaxon at the top station, and, with a sudden jerk, we began to move slowly out of the covered entrance up the side of the mountain.

After the initial jerk, we settled into an easy, gentle climb. It was as if we were being hauled up the incline by an unseen giant at the top, his massive hands pulling at the thick cable in a constant, steady rhythm, his heels dug in leaning back slightly to take the strain, up and up the 2,500 feet to the top. The view of houses slowly turned into a view of rooftops and then gradually the whole of Innsbruck began to unfold beneath our feet revealing more and more as the climb progressed until eventually, at the top, just six minutes later, we had the whole panorama spread out below us, the entire valley nestling at the feet of the Tyrolean Alps in all its breathtaking beauty.

At the top station we had the choice of going on further up.

"We could go all the way up to the Hafelekar," said Mike, consulting his guide book as we stepped out at the top. "That's 7,500 feet. There's a cable car from here to Seegrube and then another one to the Hafelekar."

"I don't know. What do you think?" I said, decisive as ever.

"Well the book recommends that you spread the stages across three separate trips to really appreciate the different view if you've got time."

"Do you think a year's enough?"

"Well it's cutting it a bit fine but I guess on balance it'll do."

"Ok, then let's slum it down here for today."

A tree-lined path led away from the funicular station along the side of the mountain offering the gentle walk Mike had been looking for combined with the stunning view of Innsbruck and the *Saile, Serles* and *Patscherkofel* mountains in the south. It was cold up on the mountain, despite the bright sunshine, and a strong wind whipped round us as we walked and admired the view. The cold made us even more conscious of the fact that we hadn't eaten since breakfast and when a picnic area appeared round a bend, wooden tables and benches set among the trees, we gratefully took the opportunity to stop.

As usual, I hadn't given any thought to my packed lunch until I was about to leave the house that morning. Consequently, all I'd been able to do was throw together some cheese sandwiches and a bar of chocolate. I'd guessed that Mike would do things properly and I half expected him to have a picnic hamper complete with a silver dinner service and several bottles of Chateau Margaux. True to form, although not contained in a picnic basket and noticeably devoid of chateau-bottled vintage wines, Mike's packed lunch put my meagre efforts to shame.

"What's all this then?" I asked as he trooped out a variety of sandwiches, a fruit-cake, several hard-boiled eggs and some apples. "They asked you to bring lunch for everybody did they?"

"No," he retorted, "but I made more than I needed because I knew you wouldn't bother to bring much."

I feigned indignation at this vile but unfortunately accurate slur on my character.

"What do you mean? Look at these wonderful wholesome cheese sandwiches. What's wrong with those?"

"Well for a start the bread is all ragged and the cheese filling looks like you tore it off in lumps with your teeth." He sat down. "I bet you cobbled those together as an afterthought just before you left the house, didn't you?"

It astounded me sometimes that we knew each other so well after just a month.

"Well I wanted them to be fresh and anyway I knew you'd have the Fortnum and Mason's picnic hamper complete with cold grouse and rare Lithuanian truffles. It didn't seem worth trying to compete."

"In that case chuck those horrible looking things away and share this instead."

"No, no, no, no, no, no, no, no yes alright then."

I dropped my, by now, rather unappetising sandwiches into a

convenient rubbish bin and joined him in his feast.

"Now isn't this better than tramping around with a gang of overgrown boy scouts," said Mike as we made inroads into the food.

"I don't know, do I? I overslept and when I got there they had gone. Remember?"

He ignored this.

"I can almost see them, you know. Over there on the top of the Patscherkofel, planting an enormous red flag with AFS on it."

"That's where they were going is it, the *Patscherkofel*?"

"Yes, I think so. Somewhere over there anyway. We didn't really want them spoiling a special day like today."

"What's so special about today? It's not your birthday is it?"

"No but tonight's the night," said Mike fervently.

"What with Chantal and Maurice, you mean?"

"Yes. This could be the start of a whole new social life with any luck."

"Could be," I replied cautiously.

"You don't seem too sure."

"Well we don't know do we? I hope it'll work out, but I don't want to be disappointed."

I was beginning to worry that we were both setting ridiculously high score by poor Chantal. It was a pity that neither of us had ever set eyes on her and this left the field clear for a whole range of personal fantasies. For my part I'd had this daydream over the last few days in which Chantal was a petite, sexy, blond bearing a striking resemblance to Brigitte Bardot. I had indulged in visions of walking into the restaurant that night, of our eyes meeting across the crowded room in the best traditions of romantic fiction and of sitting wrapped in each other for the rest of the evening, oblivious to Mike and Maurice. I was enough of a realist not to take the daydream too seriously but the seeds of anticipation and therefore disappointment were sown nonetheless. I hadn't discussed it with Mike but I was willing to bet he was harbouring similar fantasies, too. He'd certainly been keen to set up the meeting, even to the point of swallowing his pride with regard to Maurice and I thought it unlikely that he was only concerned about improving his spoken German.

"Don't you think we should go on somewhere tonight?" Mike continued, "You know a club or a disco or something?"

"I thought you didn't like discos."

"No I don't particularly."

"Well neither do I much and I'm sure as hell Maurice wouldn't be seen dead in one. Anyway we can't afford it even if we knew a club or a disco."

Mike shrugged.

"I suppose you're right. It just seems a pity only to have dinner that's all."

"We can stay in the restaurant drinking as long as we like or go on somewhere else and drink. They all stay open well after midnight."

"True. And I suppose we can always go back to someone's place for coffee after that. I just want tonight to be something special that's all, different from our normal Saturday night."

"That won't be difficult, will it? The last few Saturdays haven't exactly been one long, wild party."

"Hardly. Anyway the disco idea wasn't very bright. We don't want to frighten Chantal off the first time we meet her."

I thought about this for a moment.

"What exactly do you do while you're dancing then, if it frightens women off?"

He tapped his nose conspiratorially.

"You'll just have to wait and see, won't you?"

We continued walking through the trees until the light began to fade and the cold got the better of us and then headed back to the funicular railway. As we approached, we saw a familiar group milling around outside the station.

"Oh no," said Mike stopping abruptly in his tracks. "It's the AFS crowd.

"I thought you said they were over the other side?"

"I thought they were. What are we going to do now?

"Well I'm not going through this morning's performance again. Anyway there are no street corners to hide round here so we'll just have to put up with it."

"No, hang on. Wait a minute. Why don't we just let them go and take the next train down?"

"Oh, for goodness sake Mike! They don't even know who we are. I take it your landlady didn't issue them with identikit pictures of us. We'll just be two strangers sharing a train with them. If we keep our mouths shut they won't even know we're English. Even we should be able to manage that for six minutes."

Everything was going fine until we reached the bottom. Then, just as we were going out through the exit I tripped and without thinking said to Mike:

"I must get these soles fixed."

His eyes silently cursed me. It was too much to hope that the Association for Foreign Students in Innsbruck would let slip the opportunity of recruiting two more. A voice behind us said:

"Hey are you guys English?"

Reluctantly Mike indicated to the tall, lithe athlete behind him that we were.

"That's swell. We're American," explained the athlete unnecessarily. "You guys living here?"

"Just for a while," I answered as evasively as possible."

"Well you won't believe your luck but we're the Association of Foreign Students in Innsbruck."

Mike and I tried to look as though we couldn't believe our luck.

"We organise social events for English speaking foreigners here," he continued. "We don't get many English guys so you'd be real welcome to join us some time."

"Yes, that would be nice," Mike answered.

To my horror, the American drew out a pen and a notebook.

"Just stick your names and addresses in here and we'll be in touch."

"It's alright," I said jumping in as quickly as possible, "we picked up a leaflet about you at the Consulate. We'll pop along to your next event."

He put the pen and notebook away.

"Swell. Just do that. As I said, some English guys would be right welcome."

We were outside the building now and Mike and I prepared to make our escape as fast as we could but he started to speak again.

"Actually it's funny meeting you two fellers today. There were a couple of English guys supposed to join us this morning."

"Oh, really," said Mike hoarsely.

"Yeah, but for some reason they never turned up."

I could see incipient guilt spreading itself over Mike's features and a slight blush appearing.

"Well maybe one of them overslept," he said desperately, "and when they got there you were gone."

"Maybe," said the American, "but it's not very likely though is it? They most probably couldn't be bothered and decided they'd rather do something else instead. See you guys around."

Chapter Thirteen

That evening, bathed, refreshed and conspicuously well-dressed, Mike and I were making our way down through the cobbled streets of the Old Town towards the *Goldene Löwe*. Maurice and Chantal were meeting us inside the restaurant.

"I wonder if they're there yet," said Mike, pushing the pace so hard I was having difficulty keeping up with him. "We don't want to keep them waiting."

"It's only just on seven-thirty," I said breathlessly. "Even if they've arrived they won't have been there long. There's certainly no need to break the Olympic walking record. Come on slow down."

"Sorry," said Mike, cutting his pace to a brisk trot, "I forgot you've only got little legs."

"Talk about a man of changing moods," I said sardonically. "First of all you refuse to walk at all this morning. Then this afternoon you decide you like it after all and now you're trying to take it up professionally. We're only meeting a couple of French assistants you know, not the Queen. We don't get our heads chopped off if we're late."

Inside the restaurant, Maurice and companion were conspicuous by their absence. Mike and I took our normal places at a large round table tucked away in an alcove at the back. Without bothering to ask us the waitress brought over two large beers and greeted us with a warm *'Grüss Gott, Meine Herren'*. She placed the beers down on the table and smiled.

"I don't suppose there's much point bringing you a menu, is there?" she said with a smile. "*Cevapceici* again no doubt?"

Over the last few weeks we'd eaten *Cevapceici* till they came out of our ears. They were a kind of Yugoslavian savoury meatball, cheap, delicious and filling. We'd discovered them on our first evening at the hotel and they were a safe bet. I'd only once been adventurous and ordered an Emmental steak which was also cheap and which I'd taken to be some kind of Swiss meat dish. I'd been horrified when the waitress came back with an enormous hunk of Emmental cheese baked in breadcrumbs. It was like eating warm rubber and I'd never experimented again. With money so short I couldn't afford to make mistakes.

"Actually," said Mike, "we've got some friends joining us tonight so we'll order when they come if that's alright?"

She looked at us and winked knowingly.

"Young ladies are they?"

She took a keen interest in how we were getting on in Innsbruck.

"Only one of them unfortunately," Mike replied with feeling.

"Well don't end up fighting over her will you? And it's not good for you to drink on an empty stomach. I'll get you something to nibble on while you're waiting."

She bustled over to the bar and came back with some peanuts and crisps.

"There we go. Enjoy your beer and just give me a shout when your friends arrive."

She disappeared off towards the *Stammtisch* to take their orders for more drinks and left us to it. I looked at my watch.

"Well that's a pity isn't it?" I said taking a handful of peanuts and drawing Mike's attention back from the entrance he was watching so intently.

"What's a pity?"

"It's obvious isn't it? They got here early, saw we hadn't arrived, decided we weren't coming and went off to have dinner on their own somewhere. Still I expect we'll see them again sometime."

He almost fell for it but realized quickly I was just winding him up. He gave me one of his looks.

"I think it's more likely that she'll come in, take one look at you and then decide she'd rather go off and eat on her own. That's what I think." With this masterly piece of repartee he went back to his contemplation of the door. A few moments later he was rewarded by the entrance of Maurice and, behind him, a small, dark-haired girl wearing faded jeans and an old anorak. Chantal obviously wasn't heavily into fashionable evening wear. Maurice cast a quick glance round the restaurant, spotted us in the alcove and led Chantal towards the table.

"Now just watch out for the over-the-top formal introduction," whispered Mike as they approached. He wasn't disappointed. Maurice went straight for it.

"Gentlemen," he said stiffly, "allow me to introduce to you Mlle. Chantal Lacaze. Chantal this is Iain Moss and Mike Jensen from England."

We both decided to play the game and rose solemnly to shake her hand, bowing sharply as we did so, Mike even going as far as to click his heels in the process. Chantal was clearly delighted with this pantomime.

"How lovely to meet two real English gentlemen," she said laughing. "I now believe everything I've read about English courtesy."

We waited for her to sit down first, just to complete the game and then sat down ourselves.

The waitress noticed the new arrivals and came hurrying over with four menus. She handed one each to Chantal and Maurice and then turned to Mike and me.

"Here you are," she said placing the remaining two on the table, "you might as well have a look at them for a change as well."

She turned back to Maurice and Chantal.

"Would you like something to drink?"

"Yes, please," said Chantal, "I'd love a large beer."

I caught the flicker of surprise in Mike's eyes as she said this. I suspected he didn't quite know what to make of Chantal. Whatever fantasies we might have nurtured prior to meeting her were quickly disappearing out the window. She certainly didn't fit my Brigitte Bardot stereotype at all. In fact, she was exactly what we should have expected if we'd cared to think about it rationally - a typical student and a neither unattractive nor stunningly beautiful girl. I hoped Mike wasn't disappointed because I wasn't. I was actually secretly rather relieved that she hadn't turned out like the fantasy version. On the one hand, each meeting with her would have been a strain because I knew what I was like and I would have been falling over myself all the time trying to impress her or, worse still, too thunderstruck to be able to talk to her at all. On the other hand, and much more importantly, it would probably have driven a wedge between Mike and myself and I'd come to value his friendship.

Maurice ordered a glass of white wine and the waitress left us to choose the food.

"Right, what am I going to eat, then?" said Chantal, eyeing the vast selection on the menu. "It needs to be something cheap and filling. I'm almost broke." She looked enquiringly around the table. "Any suggestions?"

As one man Mike and I said "*Cevapceici*" and fell about laughing. Chantal, not surprisingly, was confused, obviously convinced that as well as being perfect English gentlemen we were also as mad as hatters.

"I beg your pardon?"

"*Cevapceici*," explained Mike, pronouncing the word with relish. "They're a sort of meatball from Yugoslavia. They're really good. We eat them all the time."

"And you get chips and a salad," I added. "And they only cost thirty schillings."

Chantal closed the menu.

"Well that solves that problem then. I'll have those."

"Same goes for me," said Mike. "Maurice?"

Maurice smiled condescendingly.

"Well that all sounds very splendid but I think I'd prefer something a little more traditional. I'll have the *Wurscht* and *Sauerkraut* I think."

I caught Mike's eye, silently warning him not to pick an argument, knowing that virtually everything about Maurice made his hackles rise. *Wurscht* was the Tyrolean pronunciation of *Wurst* - sausage - and Maurice pronounced the word with great relish. Just as they disagreed on virtually everything else, they had totally conflicting views on the merits of acquiring a local accent. This time Mike heeded the silent warning and let it pass, turning instead to ask Chantal about her schools. It became clear as she answered his questions that she spoke German with an ease and fluency that almost matched Mike and Maurice. Once again, I was the one struggling to keep up with the conversation.

"So if both schools are outside the town, how do you reach them?" I heard Mike ask.

"Well I get a lift out to one of them with a member of staff and I take the Postbus out to the other. It's not very convenient but it will only be for one term. I'm bringing my car back after Christmas."

I saw Mike's eyes light up at this.

"Wow. That's fantastic. You'll be able to go all over the place."

"I wasn't going to bother but since the schools are a problem anyway it's worth the hassle of driving it here from France. So next year we'll be able to go out on trips and things at weekends."

I liked the way she said we.

The waitress returned with the drinks and then stood, pen and notepad poised ready for our orders. She grinned broadly as Chantal asked for *Cevapceici*.

"I see these two have been talking to you," she said indicating Mike and me. "I don't know what they'll do when they go back to England. Probably die of starvation."

"No," said Chantal, joining in the joke at our expense, "they'll just have to go back to eating English sausages instead."

Maurice smiled mischievously.

"I think I'd rather starve," he said.

"Ah, but Maurice," said Mike, "You've not tried them with mint sauce. That turns them into a meal fit for a king.

Maurice grimaced in disgust, probably believing that with English eating habits anything was possible, and the waitress went away with our order laughing.

"I take it you two are regulars here," said Chantal.

"Regular as clockwork," Mike replied. He explained briefly about our accommodation problem when we'd arrived.

"But that's terrible," said Chantal. "How could your schools have let that happen. It's downright negligence. I had a room ready and waiting when I got here."

"But you're a girl," said Mike. "Girls have to be protected. We can look after ourselves according to the Austrians. The English girl we know also had a room arranged when she arrived. They're very old-fashioned here."

"You can say that again. You wouldn't believe the trouble I've had over wearing trousers for school. I got so fed up with it in the end I went out and bought a plain dark skirt which I couldn't afford."

"Same with us," said Mike. "We went out in the end and bought a *Dirndl* dress each. Mind you, we look very fetching, don't we, Iain?"

Chantal giggled and even Maurice managed a smile despite his usual disapproval of our 'schoolboy' humour as he called it.

As the evening wore on Maurice's smiles turned to laughter. In fact, his laughter was becoming somewhat hysterical and uncontrolled. By the time we'd finished a second carafe of wine we were all fairly drunk but Maurice particularly was very much the worse for wear. He'd become unsteady in his movements, was talking too loudly and was largely incoherent.

"I think," he slurred with difficulty, "this is the bescht evening I've had for ages. No," he shouted, and I saw the inhabitants of the *Stammtisch* look round in surprise, "this is the best evening I've EVER had." He made an expansive movement with his hand and sent his empty glass rolling off the table. He sat for a moment blinking owl-like through his thick spectacles, as if astonished at the audacity of the glass.

"It fell off the table," he said slowly. "The glass fell off the table. Why did it do that?" He thought about it a bit longer and then smiled blearily.

"I'll juscht pick it up. Excushe me."

He fell rather than leaned down to the floor and disappeared from view. There was a moment's silence followed by drunken giggling and he eventually reappeared with the glass in his hand and replaced it unsteadily on the table.

"Got it," he said unnecessarily. "I think we should order some more before it falls off the table again."

Before we could stop him, he called over the waitress who was already watching our table with some concern.

"My friends and I will partake of a glass of your finesht Cognac," he said with a lordly wave in our direction. "Served in warmed brandy balloons if you please."

The waitress looked pleadingly at Mike and me and we decided we'd better leave before Maurice did something that would make us unwelcome in the future.

"Could we just have the bill please," said Mike, "then we'll go.

There was no protest from Maurice, who suddenly seemed to have lost interest in another round of drinks. He'd turned rather pale and gone rather quiet and his head was beginning to loll forward. Fortunately he still had enough presence of mind to pull out his wallet when the bill arrived and push it across the table to Chantal. She extracted the required amount, handed it back and said quietly in French:

"Come on, *mon petit*, I think we'd better get you home." Then in German to us:

"Do you two think you could help me take him back up to Hötting on the other side of the river? We can't possibly leave him to struggle up there on his own. He'd never make it"

"Of course," replied Mike. "Do you know exactly where he lives?"

"Just about. I'm sure I can find it."

"Right, come on then let's get him up."

Mike and I took an arm each and managed to lift a now virtually lifeless Maurice to his feet. With a struggle, we got him walking after a fashion and gently guided him out of the restaurant.

The cold air outside did nothing to improve Maurice's condition, or mine for that matter, and Mike and I almost had to carry him between us. It wasn't too far but once we were over the bridge into Mariahilf it was all uphill. By the time we were halfway, Mike and I were struggling to keep him upright.

"Hell's teeth," said Mike, as Maurice stumbled for the third time and nearly fell, "I can't go on much further like this. How far's his house Chantal?"

"Well it shouldn't be too far now. His street's the one round the corner at the top of the hill. Then we need to find number 58."

"What are we going to do with him when we get him there?" I asked. "We can't just dump him on the doorstep."

"I'm tempted to dump him by the side of the road right here," mumbled Mike grumpily to me in English.

"I presume his keys are in his pocket," said Chantal. "We'll have to find them, let ourselves through the front door and put him to bed in his room."

Mike and I were open-mouthed at this.

"You can't do that," said Mike aghast.

"Of course I can. I've done this sort of thing lots of times. I was always putting people to bed back at university."

"But what about the family he lives with?"

"Alright I'll put them to bed too if you like," said Chantal merrily.

"How can you joke at a time like this? This is serious." He caught the outline of a smirk flicker across my face and rounded on me.

"You're not taking this seriously either."

"I am Mike, I promise you. I just don't see the point of having a nervous breakdown over it that's all."

Mike was not convinced but allowed Chantal to continue outlining her plan.

"You're right in that we do need to be careful about the people he lives with. It's gone midnight and they should be in bed by now. But we must make sure they don't see him like this. I get the impression they think he's terribly quiet and studious and extremely well-behaved. I don't think they'd approve of this at all."

After much struggling and cursing, we eventually got Maurice to the top of the hill and round the corner to his house. Grateful to be relieved of our burden at last we propped him up against a gate-post and watched as Chantal expertly rifled his pockets and dug out his keys.

"Right," she said, in total command now, "you two stay here and keep an eye on him while I go and open the door and try and find his room. I'll give you a signal when everything's ready."

Fortunately the house was in darkness and it looked like the family were indeed asleep. Chantal walked softly up to the front door and tried the keys one by one in the lock until she found the right one. Then quietly she opened the door and slipped inside. We waited patiently for several minutes, keeping a tight hold on Maurice until she reappeared in the doorway and waved us to bring him in.

To start with everything went fine and we negotiated Maurice up the garden path to the front door where Chantal stood with relative ease.

"His room is up on the first floor," whispered Chantal in my ear. "His name's on the door thank goodness. Just get him up there and you can leave the rest to me."

It was only once we were actually inside the house that the trouble started. Ever since we'd left the restaurant, Maurice had been lost to the world in a drunken stupor but he suddenly decided that this of all moments was the time to wake up. After an initial grunt or two he came alive and burst into a loud, drunken rendering of the *Marseillaise*. Horrified, I clapped my hand over his mouth and we stood, frozen, hardly daring to breathe, listening for any sign of movement upstairs. We could hear nothing.

"I think we got away with it," whispered Chantal.

But she spoke too soon. Just as we were about to continue the manoeuvre, there was the sound of footsteps upstairs and a door opened. A woman's voice called:

"Herr Maurice, is that you?"

No one moved, no one said a word. She called again, more urgently this time:

"Herr Maurice, Herr Maurice!"

She was silent for a moment and I thought at first that she was going to go back to bed, but then the light came on and with a sinking feeling in my stomach, I heard her coming down the stairs.

It must have been quite a shock for Frau Spätzl to be woken late at night by the strains of the French national anthem and then to come down stairs to find three complete strangers propping up her lodger. We just stood there, a motley crew, staring dumbly at the approaching storm.

"Oh God," groaned Mike helpfully.

She stopped several feet away, surveying the scene and then said in a strong Tyrolean accent:

"Herr Maurice. What is going on here? Who are these people?"

Maurice, who by now was beginning to sober up a little, tried to answer but was thwarted by my hand still clamped tightly over his mouth. I let him go.

"Theesh are my friends," he said swaying slightly, "and we've had a wonderful time. The besht time......"

Chantal interrupted him with one last ditch attempt to save the situation.

"Maurice was.. er.. taken ill. So we've brought him home. We're very sorry we disturbed you. We'll just put him to bed and then go."

She looked pleadingly at Frau Spätzl who was silent for a moment before smiling knowingly and saying:

"Oh, I see. Well that's fine then. I'll give you a hand. The two Herren can go and sit in the kitchen. I'll make us all a cup of coffee when we've settled Herr Maurice down for the night."

Totally bemused, Mike and I did as we were told and went to the kitchen while Chantal and Frau Spätzl took Maurice off to bed.

"You don't really think she bought the story about him being taken ill, do you?" I asked as Mike and I sat waiting.

"Of course not. It was obvious he was as pissed as a rat. She just wants him out of the way before she lays into us for leading him astray and breaking into her house."

"She didn't seem too put out. She said she was going to make us coffee."

"Just softening us up," said Mike gloomily, "you wait and see."

After ten minutes or so they returned laughing and chatting together and Mike and I waited nervously for the storm to break. Frau Spätzl made a fresh pot of coffee as she'd promised and then sat down with us at the table. She turned to Mike who flinched and steeled himself and said:

"And how do you like living in Austria?"

Mike blinked, not responding. I could see his mind racing as he tried to find the catch in the question. After what seemed like an age he pulled himself together.

"It's..er.. very nice," he gabbled, "I mean I.. er..like it."

"And you, mein Herr," she continued turning to me.

"Well yes," I answered equally confused, "I like it too."

She turned back to Mike again.

"Where in England do you come from?"

Momentarily Mike seemed to have forgotten where he came from but, with another superhuman effort of will, he managed to stammer out a reply. And that's how it went on. Polite vicar's tea party conversation about our jobs and our impressions of Austria and not a mention of the paralytic Frenchman upstairs. It was surreal and I found it virtually impossible to hold a sensible conversation. Chantal, on the other hand, was perfectly at ease and chatted away quite happily. I caught Mike's eye a couple of times and he looked as if he was likely to crack under the strain at any moment. Maybe that was the plan. Frau Spätzl would avoid the subject until we all broke down under the strain of waiting and confessed. Whatever was going on, I'd had enough. I finished my coffee as quickly as I could and then pointedly offered to walk Chantal home as it was getting very late. With a great sense of relief, we were shown to the door and bidden a friendly goodnight by a smiling Frau Spätzl.

As soon as we were out on the street, we both turned on Chantal.

"What the hell happened in there?" asked Mike.

"She didn't really believe he was ill, surely?" I added.

"Of course she didn't. She knew he was drunk alright," replied Chantal.

"Well why didn't she have a go at us, you know, call the police or throw Maurice out on the street or something?" Mike was obviously quite distraught at the lack of recrimination.

"Because she was pleased, that's why."

"What the hell was there to be pleased about?" I asked.

"She's very fond of Maurice, they all are. She thinks he's wonderful. But she worries about him. She thinks he works too hard and spends too much time alone with his books instead of going out and enjoying himself. Now she's seen that he's made some friends and does let his hair down occasionally she's happy for him. Simple, isn't it."

We both declined to reply to this. It had all been too much.

"Actually," continued Chantal, as we walked down the hill, "it's even better than that. I suspect that she thought he didn't like girls either. Now she thinks I'm his girlfriend. She was happy about that too."

"I don't believe it," said Mike shaking his head. "Nothing ever seems to turn out like you expect it too."

"Oh I don't know," I said, "one thing did."

"What?"

"Well you said we'd probably end up back at someone's place for coffee tonight. We certainly did that alright."

Chapter Fourteen

The weather was turning colder and winter was taking over with a vengeance making the early morning walk to school a painful one. Typically, I'd come to Innsbruck ill-prepared and I was really beginning to miss a warm pair of gloves and a scarf. These were further items to add to the shopping list for the great day when the money came. We were now in the third week of November and there was still no sign of a salary cheque. I had complained bitterly to Reiner and he had discussed the matter with the Headmaster but they were hamstrung by Austrian bureaucracy. It took time to add a new name into the system and that was that. I had opened an account at the little bank across the road weeks before but it was empty as ever, still waiting for its first infusion of real money. I was already well-known to the counter staff having been in there almost every day for the last few weeks to see if anything had been paid in without me knowing, and I was always treated with the utmost courtesy and respect. As soon as I opened the door I was greeted with a chorus of 'Grüss Gott, *Herr Professor* Moss'. A teacher, even a penniless foreign teacher was an important person in Austria. Of course, there was no problem borrowing money. Hans, Reiner and Viktor asked me almost daily if there was anything I needed but I hated borrowing money and anyway I couldn't be extravagant with other people's.

By the time I reached the school that particular morning, I was chilled to the bone and I made straight for the smokers' room where there was usually a pot of hot, strong coffee on the boil. The school staff had taken a vote on smoking in the staffroom and it had been agreed that those wishing to smoke during breaks should do so in a separate room. Only Reiner broke this rule but no one ever seemed inclined to take him to task about it. The school also had a smoking room for pupils. Anyone over sixteen with a letter from his parents giving him permission to smoke could use the room. This was another example of the school placing responsibility for a child's discipline in the hands of the parents.

As usual, the staff smoking room was empty except for Kristine

Mühlegger and Reiner. They were both incorrigible chain smokers and the main users of the room. The coffee machine had been supplied by Kristine which is why it was situated here rather than in the main staffroom. It was a kind of challenge to the non-smokers - if you want coffee you'll have to come and risk your lives in here. I greeted them in my best Tyrolean:

"*Grüss Di' Kristine, Grüss Di' Reiner.*"

"My God," said Reiner dryly, "spoken like a true yokel. You look awful this morning."

"Thank you very much, that makes me feel a whole lot better."

"My poor dear," said Kristine, "you look absolutely frozen. Here take a cigarette to be going on with and I'll get you a nice hot cup of coffee."

She pushed a packet of German cigarettes into my cold-numbed fingers and went over to the coffee machine. I liked Kristine. She was another member of the English staff and I worked in a couple of her fifth-form classes and one first form. She was a bit like a female version of Reiner, outspoken, unorthodox but a highly successful teacher. She was a little older than Reiner, in her late thirties in fact, and still extremely attractive. Her husband was a very senior local government official and a close friend of Reiner. I took one of her cigarettes and handed back the packet in exchange for a little plastic cup of very hot coffee. I didn't really smoke cigarettes, preferring my occasional small cigar, but I liked the closed intimacy of the smokers' room better than the impersonal bustle of the main staffroom and I took the occasional cigarette just to be sociable. I never inhaled them or smoked them outside that room but I just liked holding one, being part of the small group.

"Where are your gloves?" Kristine asked looking at my frozen hands. "You shouldn't walk around in this weather without a pair. And it's going to get worse you know. The snows are on their way. We can't send you back to England with only two fingers on each hand can we now?"

"Oh, I never wear gloves," I lied. I didn't want to get onto the embarrassing subject of my financial problems again if I could help it.

"Well you must. You'll need a pair for skiing anyway. You are going to ski aren't you?"

"Of course. Hans is going to take me up to the slopes as soon as the snows arrive."

"You know you also get a free week's skiing out of the school?" said Reiner.

"Well Hans did mention I'd be able to go ski camp later in the year with the pupils. When is it exactly?"

"Oh there's not just one. There are several spread over the season. The kids go off in groups, two school years at a time. It's entirely up to you which group you go with but my advice would be to go on the last one at the beginning of March. That's for the older kids, years seven and eight. You'll have more fun with them than with a bunch of whining juniors and it also gives you a chance to ski a bit first. The kids are all experts. And I'll be on that one, so will Hans and quite a few of the volleyball regulars. But as I say it's up to you."

"OK, put me down for that one."

Reiner smiled slyly.

"I already have," he said.

Before I could comment on this presumption the five-minute bell rang for the first lesson and the mad rush began to get books and papers together and get to the classrooms before the second bell. I went over to the main staffroom and sought out Frau Grindl. We were together in 7a again.

"I was going to ask you to continue going through that article on Apartheid we started last week," she said as we walked down the corridor to the classroom, "but unfortunately it bored them to tears. I thought that going through an article with you rather than me would get them more interested but I'm afraid they just don't like reading articles. Now I haven't given you a chance to prepare anything else so I'm quite happy to take the lesson myself. But if there's anything in particular you'd like to try with them then please go ahead and do so."

As it happened there was a language teaching game I had read about somewhere and I was dying to try it out. It was called 'Alibi' and was based on a courtroom cross-examination. With a good class such as 7a, who had a very high standard of spoken English, it could work quite well.

"Actually there is something I'd like to try," I told her tentatively, "but it's a bit unconventional. It's a kind of teaching game. Would you mind?"

"Does it involve noise, violence or moving the furniture around?" she asked warily.

"No," I replied. "It's a verbal game."

"Alright, I'm all for new teaching methods. Go ahead and try it."

Frau Grindl took the first five minutes of the lesson herself. She collected up the previous day's homework, handed out a reading list for the next lesson and then explained that I was going to play a game with them. This caused great excitement and a lot of chattering among the pupils but they were silenced immediately.

"This is not, however, an opportunity for you to go mad," she said threateningly. "Although conducted within the framework of a game this is a serious learning exercise. If you treat it as an excuse to misbehave, we will go back to reading newspaper articles. Is that clearly understood?"

There was a chorus of 'Yes, Frau Professor' and Else turned to me with a smile.

"OK, Iain, they're all yours."

I took my place in front of the class, the centre of attention for thirty pairs of bright, excited eyes. I hoped they weren't going to be disappointed.

The idea of the game was very simple. The teacher creates a mythical crime and a time at which it is supposed to have taken place. He then accuses two members of the class of having perpetrated the crime and sends them out of the room to make up an alibi between them detailing what they were doing before, during, and after the supposed crime. They are then brought back in one at a time and questioned by the class about their whereabouts during the incident. The object is to keep calling them in and out until a flaw appears in their respective stories and the alibi is broken. With luck the whole class participates and everyone gets to practice their spoken English while enjoying playing a game at the same time.

I spent a little while explaining the game and writing useful vocabulary up on the board then, once they'd all got the idea, I invented a bank robbery between 8 and 10 o'clock the previous night and sent two of the better pupils outside to prepare an alibi. While they were out of the room I ran briefly through the kinds of questions we need to ask when they returned and how we might go about trapping them into inconsistencies. Then, when I felt they had had long enough, I went and called in the first of the suspects.

"Would you please tell the court," I asked pompously, "where you were yesterday evening between the hours of seven and ten p.m.?"

"Yes, sir. I met my friend Johann at seven o'clock in the University Street and we went coffee to drink. When we had drinked the coffee we went to the Kinema and have seen a film. Then we walked home to the house of Johann and have played disks until eleven. Then I said him goodbye and went to my house. That is all I will tell the court, sir."

I was pleased that he was entering into the spirit of the thing. I threw the game over to the rest of the class.

"Right, he's your witness. Cross-examine him."
The questions came thick and fast probing every word of his statement. Where did he have coffee, what film did he see, how much were the tickets, what records did they play? When they were satisfied I called in witness number two and we went through the same routine again, alibi followed by questions. At first the questions were just a repeat of the first round but when these drew blanks and failed to point up inconsistencies, the class began to get clever.

"Where exactly did you sit in the cinema?" asked one pupil.

"Were you in time to see the cartoon?" asked another.

"Who arrived first at the meeting place?" questioned a third.

By the time suspect number one had been recalled and questioned for a second time, holes were beginning to appear in the alibi. One claimed they sat in the circle the other in the stalls. One saw the cartoon, the other didn't. Both arrived first at the meeting place and waited for the other. When suspect number two had been recalled for the second time the story lay in shreds and the alibi had collapsed.

I called them both in together and gravely sentenced them to ten years hard labour for bank robbery before sending them back to their seats. I just had time to ask if there were any questions arising from the game when the bell rang and the lesson ended.

"Well I never," said Else as we left the pupils behind chattering excitedly among themselves about the game, "quite extraordinary. Where on earth did you come across that?"

"In a book of language teaching games I bought in England," I told her. "Good, isn't it?"

"Excellent. I've never seen anything like that before. They spoke English almost continuously for forty-five minutes and loved every minute of it. You've a whole book of these games you say?"

"Yes, but having looked through them all I think 'Alibi' is probably the best."

"Could you bring it in? I'd like to have a look at it if I may."

"Of course. I'll try and remember to bring it with me tomorrow."

"Thank you. And thanks for the lesson, too, it was quite amazing."

We parted at the door of the staffroom and I continued on to the smokers' room walking on clouds and still glowing from the success. I couldn't wait to see Mike at lunchtime and tell him all about it.

There were about half-a-dozen people in the room this time, all gathered round the coffee machine clutching white paper cups in their hands. As I approached, I was accosted by Mannfred from the volleyball group who thrust his freshly poured cup of coffee into my hand, poured himself another and then pulled me gently to one side.

"Hey, Iain, you play football, don't you?"

After my last exhibition, I was tempted to say 'no, but I show off a lot' but I didn't know how to say it in German anyway so I just nodded.

"How do you feel about playing in the big match on Sunday?"

"What big match?"

"Teachers versus pupils, five-a-side in the gym, you know grudge match, local derby and so forth. We need a striker."

It sounded alright. I hadn't played five-a-side football for ages and there was never much to do on a Sunday afternoon. The only problem was my position.

"I'd love to play but I'm not really a striker. I'm fine just kicking around with no opposition but I'm no good in a match. I'm really a goalkeeper. Is that any good to you?"

Mannfred was thoughtful for a moment.

"Ok," he said, "why not. We can move Johannes out into the

defence and put Hans in the forward line. He's convinced he's a world-class striker anyway. Can you be at the school by four-thirty on Sunday?"

"No problem. I'll look forward to it."

"That's great. Thanks a lot. I'll just go and sort out the others. See you later."

He disappeared in the direction of the main staffroom crossing paths with Reiner who was just coming through the door. He lit another cigarette from the butt in his hand and made straight for me.

"Hi," he said, "I've just been talking to Else and the headmaster. She's been going on about some lesson you did this morning. Something to do with sending kids out of the room and then interrogating them about what they've been doing out there. It sounds weird to me personally but the Head seemed quite impressed. Of course some people are easily pleased. Still I suppose that means that we won't be getting rid of you just yet."

The bell rang for the next lesson.

"You're with Kristine now in 1c aren't you?"

I nodded, not sure how to take his previous remarks.

"Well you'd better go and find her then, or you'll be late."

Kristine was waiting for me outside the classroom.

"You look dazed," she said, "what's the matter?"

"I think Reiner just told me I'm doing alright. I'm still in shock."

She looked at me with mock concern, put her hand on my forehead and tut-tutted a few times.

"Oh dear me," she said. "Not well at all. Delirious I'd say. I told you not to walk around without gloves on. Now come on and stop fantasising. We've got work to do with these little monsters."

The little monsters served to bring me back to earth again with a bump. Teaching junior classes was far and away the most difficult and frustrating part of my job at the school involving endless repetition of basic texts and simple question and answer routines based on picture books. It was really a waste of my time. Making conversation with teenagers capable of putting together and understanding English sentences was interesting, worthwhile and well within the capabilities of any native speaker. Eliciting responses from children with a basic vocabulary of less than a hundred words and only a passing acquaintance with English grammar was boring, soul-destroying and incredibly difficult. It was a job for a highly skilled professional teacher which I wasn't. I always managed to confuse them with words they didn't know and grammatical forms they'd not yet come across and I always spoke too fast. Unlike the pupils further up the school, the juniors dreaded my lessons. I could see them during a question and answer session positively quaking with fear, waiting for their turn to be made to look stupid when I fired some incomprehensible burst of English at them. Kristine insisted it was good for them to see 'English in action' and that it 'fed their curiosity about the English as a people'. I suspected that all it was in fact doing was creating a race of Anglophobes.

In this particular lesson, I reached new heights of incompetence. Fate had obviously decided that I had had enough euphoria for one day and that it was now time to bring me down a peg or two. First of all, I went through the lesson out of sequence, beginning to ask questions before the pupils had read the text aloud. As always, they knew this wasn't right and began whispering to each other and looking at Kristine as if to say 'he's got it wrong again Miss'.

Then I based a whole series of questions on a phrase that I'd actually taught another first-year class, not this one, causing even more chaos. And finally the culmination came when I unthinkingly introduced the past tense into my questions. I'll never forget all those frightened little faces trying to answer questions in a tense they didn't know, surreptitiously looking up 'were' and 'was' in their dictionaries when they thought I wasn't watching. Eventually, Kristine decided it had gone far enough and stepped in to take over the rest of the class herself much, I'm sure, to the relief of her class.

As we left the classroom at the end of the lesson I apologised profusely to Kristine for wasting her lesson. I felt particularly stupid after what I'd told her at the beginning about Reiner. Eventually, she stopped walking and put both hands on my shoulders.

"Iain," she said, "I'm going to be serious with you once and only once and give you some advice. That is if you're ready to listen."

I indicated that I was.

"You're not a bad teacher in your own way, at least when it comes to conversation classes. You have a knack of being able to keep the conversation going come what may. In fact, I sometimes think I could give you a telephone directory and you'd still be able to keep a discussion going on it for forty-five minutes. But I would think very carefully before taking up teaching as a career. I say that for two reasons really. Firstly, day-to-day teaching is soul-destroying for a creative teacher. There is just too little freedom within the constraints imposed by exams and often far too little enthusiasm in the pupils to make it really fulfilling. Secondly, one of your strengths is looking for perfection in every lesson but your weakness is blaming yourself when you don't achieve it. Most teachers are happy to accept one good lesson among a string of mediocre ones. You wouldn't be. In your own eyes you'd only ever be as good or as bad as your last lesson. If you must teach, do it in a university or college or even teach adults, but above all learn to accept that not every lesson can be a great personal experience and when they don't work it's not always your fault."

She took her hands away and gave me a big smile.

"OK," she said, "that's it. I promise I'll never lecture you again. Let's go and have a coffee and a cigarette. You look like you need it."

I had five classes on the timetable for that day and after the fourth Reiner grabbed me in the corridor.

"Hi," he said, "I'm glad I've found you. The Headmaster wants to have a word with you sometime this morning."

"What about?"

"I don't know. He's probably just going to do his 'how are you settling in' routine. We might as well go along now and get it over with. It won't take long."

"Alright then."

We went back to the staffroom to drop off our books and then through the door into the secretary's office.

"The Head would like to see myself and *Herr Professor* Moss," Reiner told Frau Hinckle. "Could you find out if it's convenient now?"

"Of course, *Herr Professor*. I'll just go and see."

She disappeared into the inner sanctum and we waited until the door opened again and the secretary reappeared.

"The Head will see you both now," she said. "Please come this way."

This was only my second visit to the Headmaster's study and the scene was much the same as on the first occasion. Behind the large, highly-polished desk sat a small highly-polished man in a dark three-piece suit. With customary formality, he rose to shake my hand and then motioned us to sit down before taking his seat behind the desk again.

"Thank you for coming to see me. This won't take a moment." He smiled conspiratorially. "I've got some rather good news for you."

He reached down behind his desk, unlocked a drawer and pulled out a small white envelope. Even before he told me what it was I'd guessed and a mixture of excitement and relief flooded through me.

"I have here a cheque for 6,000 schillings in part payment of your first month's salary. It is, in fact, very nearly all of it. The rest will be paid into your bank account along with your next salary payment. After that you will receive a regular monthly remuneration as per your contract. Now if you would be so kind as to sign this piece of paper," he handed me a form headed 'Receipt of Salary Advance', "then the cheque is yours."

Hurriedly, my hand still shaking from the excitement, I signed my name on the piece of paper and handed it back. In return he handed over the precious white envelope and said:

Congratulations, Herr Moss. You're now officially on the books."

I thanked him profusely as if it was a personal gift from the Headmaster himself and then, still tightly clutching the envelope, I got up with Reiner and left. Once back in the staffroom I immediately ripped it open, hardly daring to believe that I really had some money at last, but there it was, a cheque for six thousand schillings made out in my name.

"Six thousand schillings, Reiner," I shouted, holding it in the air like a trophy, "I thought it was never going to come."

"How much of it do you owe?" asked Reiner.

"Two thousand to Hans, plus whatever he wants as rent for the first month. But even if he wants a thousand that still leaves me three and that hasn't got to last very long."

"So I suppose your one desire now is to go and blow the whole lot on drink, women and tasteful souvenirs of Innsbruck."

"No, not at all. I'll leave the women until next month."

"And I guess what you'd really like is to go and cash the cheque and start right away."

"Well I would but I've got a class with you, remember?"

"I know. But the chances of getting any useful work out of you this morning have just plummeted. You'd better take the rest of the day off and go and get it out of your system."

I was delighted. The cheque was already beginning to burn a hole in my pocket."

"That's great. Thanks very much. But are you sure you can cope without me?"

Reiner rose to the bait beautifully.

"Of course I can bloody cope. Unlike the rest of my staff, apparently, I can still hold a class for forty-five minutes without you being there to hold my hand, thank you very much."

He gathered up his books and prepared to go to his next class but as he was about to leave, he turned back.

"By the way," he said, "before you go off and paint the town red on government money, it might be a good idea to leave Hans a cheque for what you owe him. That way you won't be tempted to spend it."

I nodded. I'd planned to do that anyway.

"Right then have fun."

"I will. And thanks, I do appreciate it."

Over at the bank, I was greeted with the usual chorus of *'Grüss Gott, Herr Professor'* and one of the senior clerks left his position behind the counter and came forward to meet me.

"I'm terribly sorry, *Herr Professor*," he said apologetically, "there is still no sign of your money."

"That's OK," I said, "I have it here." Like a magician producing a rabbit from a hat, I took the cheque from my pocket with a flourish.

"Excellent, excellent. And presumably you would like to pay the cheque into your account and then draw some money on it?"

"Yes please."

"Fine. If you would be so kind as to come with me, I will do it for you."

He was obviously pleased to be able to do something positive for me at last and the whole operation was over in moments. All I had to do was tell him how much I wanted, sign two pieces of paper and there it was at last, two thousand schillings in crisp new notes in my hand to do with as I pleased.

"Thank you very much indeed," I said. "The money will be paid direct into my account from now on."

"It's our pleasure, *Herr Professor*, thank you."

There had been no queuing and no fuss and five minutes after I'd entered, I was out again, the chorus of *Auf Wiedersehen Herr Professor* still echoing behind me and my money safely tucked away in my pocket.

It was still too early to meet Mike for lunch so I decided to buy some provisions and take them back to the house before going into town. My shopping this time was a fine example of senseless, extravagant buying, for which I was completely unrepentant, and I arrived home loaded down with expensive Swiss liqueur chocolate, a bottle of schnapps, two whole salamis, some English brand Earl Grey tea and an enormous black-forest gateau.

"My goodness," said Ingrid, who was just coming out of her room as I struggled through the front door, "are you planning a party?"

"No," I said, putting down my bag and closing the door, "I've just been paid and I'm celebrating by being deliberately extravagant."

"Oh I see. You're into the 'all the things I wanted but couldn't afford' syndrome. Well have fun won't you."

"I am, I am. And if you want any salami or black-forest gateau just help yourself. I'll never be able to eat all this on my own. I'll leave it in the larder.

Ingrid laughed.

"Ok. Maybe we'll take you up on that."

After the initial problems, I was beginning to settle down quite well in the house. Rolf and Ingrid in particular had been very kind to me. I had eventually started to accept invitations to eat with them and had benefited both from the opportunities to speak German and the introduction to home-cooked Austrian food. They also had a television, the thing I missed most about Axams, and had made it clear that I was always welcome to come in and watch with them. A few days earlier Rolf, Herbie and I had spent a pleasant evening watching a football match while drinking far too much of a particularly lethal brand of Japanese whisky that Herbie was partial too. I had bought the schnapps as my contribution next time it happened. In return for all the kindness, I volunteered for the occasional stint of baby-sitting as and when required.

I offloaded my provisions in the kitchen and then went to dump my books in my room. I had done a lot of work on the room in the weeks since I moved in, eager, like all new occupants, to stamp my personality on my surroundings. There were now posters and prints on the walls and my books carefully arranged on the bookshelves. I'd also moved the furniture around, using the size of the room to create separate living and sleeping areas. But my pride and joy was the oven and I'd taken the trouble to clean and polish it till the green porcelain positively shone. I had taken delivery of a large bag of brick coal and brought a pile of kindling logs up from the cellar and I now had the knack of keeping it burning. It was a masterpiece of engineering ideally suited to the size of the room and the winter climate in Innsbruck, conserving and radiating heat far better than an open fire. It was tremendously soothing on a bitterly cold night to sit warm and cosy in the room listening to the muffled crackling behind the solid cast-iron door and the howling wind outside. My only problem with it was the difficulty in controlling the temperature. If I wanted the room to be warm when I got up in the morning I had to be prepared to boil when I got into bed.

As I walked through the bustling lunchtime crowds towards our meeting place in the Old Town it occurred to me that I'd rather taken it for granted that Mike had been paid too. If he hadn't it was going to be rather a letdown since I'd planned to spend that afternoon on the shopping-spree we'd promised ourselves for so long. I couldn't reasonably go off and do it on my own and anyway it wouldn't be half as much fun. I needn't have worried however. As soon as he saw me coming, he went into a strange ape-like routine of smiles, waves and thumbs-up signs which made their point clearly enough.

"Did you get paid?" he shouted as soon as I was within earshot.

"Six thousand," I called back.

"Same as me. Isn't it magic?"

We held up further conversation until I arrived next to him.

"Have you spent any of it yet?" he asked.

I told him about my miniature shopping-spree and the unexpected free period.

"I was only in for the first two lessons," he said, "so I had time to stock up the fridge for a fortnight and take my suit to the dry-cleaners at last."

It's very strange what you dream of being able to do if you had the money when you're broke. Mike had been looking forward to getting his suit cleaned for weeks.

At the *Mensa* we kept an eye out for Maurice but finished the meal without catching sight of him. He had been rather elusive since that meal with Chantal and we suspected he had been deliberately avoiding us. The few times we had bumped into him he had been embarrassed and self-conscious, eager to get away as quickly as possible. Each time he had feigned other engagements when we suggested going out together. He was apparently ashamed of what had happened and unable just to laugh it off as Mike and I would have done. We'd realised that there was nothing we could do except be patient and give him time to get over it. Chantal, too, after the promising start, had been something of a disappointment. We had been out with her twice since the first meeting but always on a weekday. Both weekends she had been to stay with French friends also working as assistants, one in Vienna the other in Southern Germany, and although we accepted that it was sensible to travel while she had the opportunity, it did leave Mike and me on our own again.

By sheer chance, however, we stumbled across Maurice in the cafe across the road. He was sitting at a table all by himself tucking into two enormous cream cakes. For once we both pleased to see him and he even seemed quite glad to see us. It didn't occur to me at the time, but a few weeks previously I would have been very annoyed to find Maurice there since it would have meant forcing myself to speak German. Now it didn't even cross my mind. Speaking German almost continuously at home and at school I now slipped into it quite naturally. Curiously, though, I was still convinced I hadn't improved much at all since coming to Austria

"Hi, Maurice," I said, "we don't often see you in here."

"I got paid this morning," he replied indistinctly through a mouthful of cake, "six thousand schillings. I thought I'd celebrate."

"So did we," said Mike. "Do you mind if we join you?"

"No, not at all." He motioned towards two of the empty chairs at the table and we sat down. Mike called the waitress over and we ordered a coffee each before going off and choosing the most expensive cakes we could find from the display stand in the entrance to the shop. For ten minutes or so there was nothing to be heard from our table except the sounds of coffee being drunk and cakes being devoured, until, finally, we all sat back replete and contented.

"It's great to have money again," said Maurice, pushing away his plates. "That's why I haven't been going out much recently, really, you know, what with money being short and everything."

He looked at us expectantly, waiting to see how we would react. Of course neither Mike nor I believed this for a moment but we were more than happy to let him write off the past few weeks in this way if that made him feel better.

"It's been like that with us too," said Mike, "but perhaps we can all start going out a bit more now."

"Yes, I'd like that," answered Maurice. "I can't make Saturday this week but why don't we go out to dinner on Sunday for a change?"

"Well, I'm playing football in the afternoon against a team of pupils," I said. "I don't know how long it'll go on so I could be late. But I'll definitely make it."

"Well I had planned to run a marathon and scale the *Hungerburg* on Sunday afternoon," said Mike ironically, always ready to poke fun at what he considered an unhealthy obsession with physical exercise, "but I guess it can wait until another day. So Maurice and I will meet at seven-thirty and go straight to the restaurant and you come along whenever you can. Why don't we eat at *Churrasco*? The atmosphere's good and we can afford it now."

I admired Mike's tact in avoiding the *Goldene Löwe*.

"What about Chantal," I asked. "Is she around this weekend?"

Maurice shook his head.

"She's going to Vienna again," he said.

Mike and I were desperate to go off and spend some more money and we explained to Maurice about the game we'd been playing for the last month.

"We're going into the centre and then over to my part of the town," said Mike, "to buy Iain's lighter and my coffee-maker. Do you fancy coming with us?"

Maurice thought for a moment.

"I ought to do some work really," he said hesitantly, "but funnily enough I've always wanted one of those little espresso coffee pots, you know, the metal ones that you stand on the stove."

"They sell them in this shop," said Mike, the voice of temptation.

Maurice wavered and then succumbed.

"Alright then. Why not?" he said decisively. "I think I deserve a present too."

"Let's go then," said Mike. "There's no point in having all this money unless we go out and spend it in style."

By the middle of the afternoon, we had done just that, visiting virtually every shop between the river and the Pradl district where Mike lived, making small purchases here and there on the way in addition to the main purchase we had each settled on. As we stood outside the final shop, tired and flushed from our exertions, laden down with bags, Maurice suddenly shouted:

"Hey, look at that."

Mike and I turned in the direction of Maurice's pointing finger and both gasped when we saw what he'd noticed. All day the town had been surrounded by mists, completely obscuring the mountain ranges beyond. Now, suddenly, the mist around the 'Nordkette' had lifted and there, breathtakingly beautiful, were the mountains, no longer shades of green and brown but a brilliant white, clad in their new coats of clean bright snow. For several minutes, we just stood there, spellbound by the speed of the transformation, lost in the unexpected beauty of it all.

Finally, Mike recovered his voice and whispered to me:

"I reckon that's a sign, you know, an omen. Everything's going to be different from now on. Everything's going to change for the better. You see if I'm not right."

As I continued drinking in the glorious scene, I couldn't help believing he might indeed be right.

Chapter Fifteen

The next Sunday afternoon I set off from the house at half-past three, sports bag in my hand, looking forward to a game of football at the school. The match wasn't due to start until four but I wanted plenty of time to get changed and warmed up and I had nothing better to do on a Sunday afternoon. The weather had turned increasingly colder and the locals were expecting snow in the valley at any time but the sun still shone brightly overhead and at least I now had the benefit of warm, new gloves, purchased during the shopping spree. And anyway a nice quiet game of football with a few of the staff and pupils would warm me up quite nicely.

It was a bit of a shock when I arrived at the school. As I approached the gym the noise of shouting and cheering was deafening. A quick glance through the windows showed a game already in progress and what looked like half the school spread out round the sides of the gym spectating. Somewhat confused, I made my way to the staff changing room where I found Reiner.

"Hi, Iain," he said cheerfully, "you're here nice and early. We've got a while to wait yet."

"What on earth's going on in there? I thought it was just us against the school team."

"Oh no," he explained, "today's the annual school tournament. Every class from the fourth-year upwards fields a team and they battle it out between them on a knockout basis. We play the winning team at the end. It's a school tradition. Didn't anybody explain what we were doing?"

I was horrified.

"No they bloody didn't," I said shrilly. "You mean to tell me that I've got to go out there and perform in front of that lot?"

"Oh don't worry. They love it."

"I bet they do. It's me I'm concerned about. I'm not used to playing in front of an audience. If I make a mess of it, I'll be a laughing stock."

"No you won't. It's just a bit of fun. Come on calm down. It

160

doesn't matter how well you play. They'll love you just for taking part. Go and get changed. It'll take your mind off it."

Needless to say, it didn't take my mind off it at all. My stomach was churning with nerves and I felt physically sick. By the time the staff team had gathered together and the whistle had blown signalling the end of the final school challenge match, I was a nervous wreck.

"Oh hell," said Mannfred, keeping watch round the door, "we're playing 7c. There are some hard little bastards in that team. Oh well, let's go and face the music lads."

As we formed a line and Mannfred led us out into the gym I felt like an F.A. Cup finalist going down the tunnel at Wembley. As we appeared there was a deafening roar followed by a sudden lull as I came onto the playing area which gave way to a chant which was taken up immediately all around the gym. It sounded like my name they were chanting only with something added to the end. Hans, who was behind me, put his hand on my shoulder and leaned forward.

"Hear that," he said, "they're calling for you."

"But what are they calling?" I asked him.

"Mossl, Mossl," he answered with a smile. "It's an affectionate diminutive. It's your nickname in the school. Didn't you know?"

I was surprised and flattered. I'd had no idea at all that I had a nickname.

Right from the start the kids were outrageously biased in my favour and I could do nothing wrong. Every time I even so much as touched the ball there was loud cheering, clapping and chanting and after a while I forgot my nerves and began to enjoy it immensely. Once I really got into the swing of it I just let go completely and hammed it up outrageously. By the end of the first half, I was making every save look spectacular, diving unnecessarily to catch or deflect low balls to the accompaniment of shrieks of delight from the spectators. So much so that at half-time, handing me a small paper cup of orange juice, Reiner said with a sardonic smile:

"Are you sure you can stay upright long enough to drink this?"

In the second half the long hard tournament began to tell on the school team and Reiner eventually broke through and scored putting the staff one-nil in front. It stayed that way right until the closing minutes when one of the school forwards made a last ditch break down towards my goal. The defence, who had gone too far forward, were taken by surprise and he went straight past them looking almost certain to score. I watched as he bore down on me knowing there was very little I could do apart from wait for the shot when suddenly Hans, who had been chasing him, grabbed the boy round the waist, pulled him away from the ball, and tapped it back to me grinning. There were howls of outrage from the spectators, followed by a chant of 'penalty, penalty' and a huge cheer when the referee pointed to the spot.

It was a Boy's Own Paper scenario really - the final minute of the game and the young fresh-faced goalkeeper, newly promoted to the first team, standing as the only barrier to the opposition stealing the game from his team's grasp. Fortunately it was also a very badly taken penalty, hit with too little force at about waist height a couple of feet to my right. Every right-handed goalkeeper loves a ball just there and it was the easiest thing in the world to dive across those two feet and catch the ball with two hands. The crowd erupted and the chant 'Mossl, Mossl' was loud enough to lift the roof. The fact that I could just as easily have walked the two feet and caught it didn't seem to have occurred to them. The final whistle went almost immediately afterwards and the staff had won the match for the first time in five years.

There was a small presentation ceremony after the match which was another part of the tradition. Five small boxes were placed in the middle of the gym and we each stood on one while our opposite number from the school team presented us with a small footballing medal and two miniature bottles of champagne. Following everyone else's lead I handed back one of my bottles to the presenter. Standing there on my box, holding my medal and listening to the cheering and chanting of the spectators, I felt like an Olympic athlete accepting a Gold medal for Britain. I couldn't help thinking at the same time about what Kristine had said a few days before about highs and lows. I respected her views but in my case I had to disagree. I needed the highs, the feeling of elation and achievement. For me that was what made life worthwhile. One good high was enough to wipe out any number of feelings of depression and failure in the past.

I was still on top of the world when I arrived at the restaurant just after eight. I was also very slightly drunk having been out for a celebration drink with the rest of the staff team. I had left Reiner almost paralytic. We had played the Austrian version of Colonel Puff with glasses of wine only Reiner had insisted on having his glass refilled with schnapps each time. The game involved each person present performing a set series of actions in sequence dictated by the game master. If a mistake was made you had to down the contents of your glass in one. Although normally an expert, Reiner was off-form for once and ended up drinking several large glasses of schnapps straight down in quick succession. From that point onwards it was a vicious circle. The drunker he got, the more mistakes he made and the more he had to drink. Not surprisingly, he was soon out of his mind. In between turns he had begun to talk loudly and emotionally about the wonderful teaching staff he had working for him, how loyal and supportive they were and how they would stick by him through thick and thin. When I'd tentatively mentioned that I had to go, he'd hit the roof, ranting on almost incoherently about my treachery and how I was unfit to have the honour of working for him. The last I'd seen of him, he was standing in the entrance to the bar, clutching a doorpost for support, shouting down the road that I could consider myself fired.

Mike and Maurice had also been drinking while they waited for me to arrive. As they saw me approaching, Mike called over the waiter and when I reached the table he stood up and offered me his hand.

"*Herr Doktor*," he said with mock seriousness, "how terribly, terribly good of you to honour us with your presence. May I introduce *Herr Professor* Vissan from the Sorbonne?"

Maurice in turn stood up, gave a little bow of the head and a click of the heels and shook my hand.

"It is a great pleasure to meet you *Herr Doktor* and so kind of you to give up your time to see us."

I cottoned on very quickly that this pantomime was for the benefit of the waiter who was now staring goggle-eyed at us and joined in with gusto.

"Not at all, my dear *Herr Professor*, not at all", I said pompously. "It's always a pleasure to dine with two of the greatest minds in

Europe." I turned back to Mike. "The Prime Minister sends his best wishes old chap. He'd like you to spend the weekend with him at Chequers next time you're in England."

"Ah dear old Jim," said Mike. "It would be splendid to see him again."

I prepared to sit down but was forestalled by the waiter as he flew past me in a blur of light and pulled the chair out.

"Allow me, Herr Doktor," he said obsequiously. Then, when I was comfortably seated:

"May I fetch you something to drink, Herr Doktor?"

"I'll have a beer please and be as quick as you can, there's a good chap. Flying always gives me such a thirst."

"Certainly, Herr Doktor. Right away, Herr Doktor."

With a little bow, he rushed off to fetch my drink.

"What on earth was all that about," I asked as soon as he was out of earshot.

"We've been having trouble with that one," said Mike laughing. "As soon as he realized we were foreign he started getting cheeky, you know, pretending not to understand and bringing the wrong things. We decided to get our own back. The Austrians are always impressed by titles."

This had happened to Mike and me a number of times in restaurants. For some reason, some Austrians, particularly shop-keepers and waiters, objected to 'tourists' who spoke German. Their standard response was persistently to misunderstand until they'd destroyed your confidence and then conduct the rest of the exchange in English. If it had only happened to me, I would have accepted that they really didn't understand, but it happened to Mike too and he spoke excellent German with only the smallest trace of an English accent. In other European countries the opposite was true. If you made an effort to speak their language, even badly, people responded much better to you. I'd mentioned it to Reiner eventually, after it had happened to us a few times.

"I think you'll find it's mainly the English and Americans who get that treatment," he'd said. "You lot have been coming over here so long demanding we speak English that in the eyes of some people you've forfeited the right to know German. And anyway there's always been a strangely ambivalent attitude to tourists among the people who make a living out of them. They're grateful for the income but resent foreigners coming in and making like they own the place. You're not a tourist but the average waiter doesn't know that and he treats all foreigners the same."

For once, that evening, we had no more trouble and after our little pantomime, we were given excellent service and treated with the utmost courtesy. My only problem was keeping a straight face when he called me *'Herr Doktor'* which he did frequently.

The meal was excellent and the surroundings were pleasant but we all agreed that there was still something missing. It just seemed to be so difficult to meet new people socially.

"Chantal's been the biggest disappointment, really," said Mike, sipping at his wine. "I had high hopes after that first meeting but it just doesn't seem to have worked out. I mean, I'm not knocking you two or anything but it would be nice to have a few more people around and especially some female company."

"I don't think she's deliberately avoiding us," said Maurice. "It's just that the opportunity to travel is too good to miss. I'm sure she enjoyed that evening in the *Goldene Löwe*."

"Yes, I know," said Mike, "I appreciate there's nothing personal but it still doesn't help us does it? Anyway I left her a note through the door telling her what we were doing tonight just in case she wanted to come when she got back from Vienna. She could at least have popped in for a drink and said hello."

"What about Jane and Gerhardt?" I asked. "We've hardly seen them since we arrived. They must know a hell of a lot of people."

"That's precisely the problem," replied Mike morosely. "They're too busy seeing other people to go out with us."

I persevered.

"What about you Maurice? One of your schools is all girls. There must be lots of nice female teachers there, you know, someone who might want to come out with us one evening?"

Maurice gave this some thought for a while.

"Well there is a young French teacher I work with called Helga. She's said a couple of times that we ought to get together for a drink one weekend."

"Have you got her telephone number?" asked Mike eagerly.

Maurice took out his diary and flicked through it.

"Yes, I have," he said hesitantly.

"Give her a ring then. Now."

"Now? But it's ten o'clock on a Sunday evening. She won't want to come out now."

"She might," Mike insisted. "And anyway you've got nothing to lose by trying, have you?"

Maurice was clearly reluctant but finally gave in.

"Alright. I'll give it a try. But I bet you she says no."

Maurice was wrong. Helga was delighted to accept our invitation and fifteen minutes later she was sitting at our table in the restaurant ordering a large carafe of red wine. She was a little older than us but not much and small, dark and attractive with laughing green eyes.

"What a lovely surprise," she said as the waiter left. "There am I sitting at home, bored to tears and gasping for a drink when Maurice rings. I hate Sundays."

"So do we," said Mike, "that's why we decided to come out for dinner."

"Well I think it's a wonderful idea. We should do it more often. Can I take one of your cigarettes?"

"Of course," said Mike, "help yourself."

He offered her the box and she took one. Self-consciously I lit it for her with my new lighter.

"Oh, that's heaven," she groaned, inhaling the smoke. "That's the first one I've smoked for two days. I've been tearing my hair out. I'll go and get a box later. I'm fed up with trying to give up. It just makes me miserable and life's just too short to be miserable."

She took a second puff, moaning in ecstasy again, then drained her glass and poured another. I found it difficult to imagine her being miserable. She positively radiated fun and enjoyment of life. She raised her glass again.

"I don't think this carafe's going to last very long," she said.

Twenty minutes later Chantal arrived.

"I'm glad you're still here," she said breathlessly, taking off an old, faded duffle-coat several sizes too large. "I just this minute got back and found Mike's note."

"Great," said Mike. "We'd almost given you up for the evening. I'll get you a glass."

"No, no," said Chantal. "Stay there. I'll get it." She went off and hung up her coat, collected a glass from the bar and returned to the table. While Maurice introduced her to Helga, Mike poured her a glass of wine.

"It looks like I was right about the wine," said Helga, eyeing the nearly empty carafe.

"Just what I was thinking," I said. "Anyone object if I order another one?"

"Feel free," said Mike.

Maurice wasn't so keen.

"I'm fine," he said, indicating his almost full glass. "But don't let me stop you." He was obviously playing it carefully after the last time.

"Well, I'm not drinking any more until I've had something to eat," said Chantal. "I'm starving."

"So am I," agreed Helga. "And anyway it's bad manners in Austria to let someone eat on their own. I wouldn't mind a goulash soup."

"Ok. I'll have that too."

Despite the fact that we'd eaten a full meal not long before Mike, Maurice and I decided to join them.

"It might help soak up some of this alcohol," said Mike.

"It'll take more than a bowl of goulash soup to soak up what we'll have drunk by the end of the evening," I told him. "Especially me. I've been drinking since six o'clock."

"That's alright," said Maurice shyly. "We'll carry you home and put you to bed. It's all part of the service."

Chantal smiled and put her arm round him. We were all relieved that at last felt he could joke about that evening. Having broken the barrier, there was no stopping him and he went on to tell Helga the whole story, with help from us on the bits he couldn't remember. Helga was delighted.

"Well I never," she said grinning broadly. "I never knew you had it in you."

By midnight the restaurant was beginning to clear and the staff were preparing to close up for the night.

"I think they'll be chucking us out soon," said Helga. "Why don't you all come back to my place for a nightcap? I've got the car outside."

We all wrestled briefly with the prospect of an eight o'clock start the next morning but soon gave up the struggle. Only Maurice voiced any real doubts about whether it was sensible and Helga soon quashed his objection.

"You've got nothing to worry about, have you? You're with me in the first lesson and I shan't tell anyone if you miss it. You've got no excuse at all for not coming."

That settled the matter and we paid the bill and then piled into Helga's car for the short trip back to her flat not far from the station.

It wasn't until two o'clock in the morning that we discovered Helga had a flatmate. As a record blared out from the stereo speakers and we talked loudly while sipping Black Label whisky, a small bleary-eyed figure in a dressing gown appeared in the doorway and said sleepily:

"Hello. Are we having a party?"

"Yes dear," said Helga. "Come and have a drink."

Being woken in the middle of the night and offered a glass of whisky would have thrown most people but poor Lisa accepted it with great equanimity. I suspected it was the kind of thing you had to get used to if you shared a flat with Helga. She took the proffered drink and came and joined us in the lounge.

For hours we sat and drank and talked and listened to music, comfortable in the warm dimly-lit sitting-room. I had been drinking since early that evening but the food seemed to have protected me from the worst effects and I was just pleasantly, happily, consciously drunk. I felt as if I had just broken through a barrier I had been trying to penetrate for so long. At last, after having believed that I would never be able to speak German well, after hiding behind Mike's command of the language since I arrived in Innsbruck, I realised that I had acquired a basic fluency without ever really being aware of it. The alcohol had taken away my inhibitions and I had spoken good, reasonably fluent German for several hours without stopping in mid-sentence to search desperately for a word and without making horrendous, basic, grammatical errors. When Lisa finally said at one point, after a long involved discussion on teaching methods, "You speak German very well, you know", I could have kissed her. I still had a strong English accent, I still made mistakes but I had made the first big breakthrough and that was success in its own way. On top of that we'd made some Austrian friends at last and there was now a small glimmer of hope on the social horizon.

I went to bed that night at five o'clock, tired, drunk and happy. I was woken by the alarm two hours later, still tired, still a little drunk and very definitely not happy. My head hurt, my eyes would hardly stay open and I had the prospect of teaching at the school for the next five hours to contend with. The warm glow in my stomach prompted by the events of the previous day was rapidly giving way to a hollow nervous feeling as I remembered I hadn't done any preparation for my first lesson with Kristine.

By the time I reached the smokers' room at the school I was beginning to feel a bit more human but my face still betrayed my night on the tiles.

"Bloody hell," said Kristine as I walked through the door, "what on earth have you been up to? No, on second thoughts, don't tell me. I don't really think I want to know."

"I went to a party," I said quietly. "Do you think I could have some coffee?"

She poured me a cup from the machine leaving out the milk.

"I think you'd better take it black this morning," she said. "And you'll have to be quick, too. The bell's about to go."

As if determined to prove her right, the bell rang almost immediately and I only had time for one desperate sip before it was time to go and face the ravening hordes.

As we walked down the corridor Kristine turned to me.

"Well, young sir. What wonders are you going to delight us with this morning?"

I thought desperately, racking my brains for some topic I could talk cogently about for forty-five minutes. It was no good. My brain had seized up. In the end, I simply turned back to her.

"Kristine," I said, "you don't by any chance happen to have a telephone directory handy, do you?"

Chapter Sixteen

"Right," said Hans, "before you do anything else, kick the snow off your boots against one of those stone pillars over there."

Obediently, I did as I was told.

"Now," he continued, "lay your skis out flat on the ground and I'll show you how to put them on."

It was the last Sunday in November and Hans had decided it was time I learned to ski. As yet there had been no snow in the town itself, but it had been falling heavily in the mountains and Hans wanted me to enjoy as much of the season as possible. He had picked me up in his car at seven in the morning, hoping to put in a full day, and driven up to the village of Mutters about six kilometres from Innsbruck. From there we had taken the long swinging gondola ride up to the *Mutterer Alm* ski slopes. He had chosen the *Mutterer Alm* because of its one long gentle slope stretching all the way down into the village and because it was serviced by the gondola. Not only would I be able to ski uninterrupted for long periods but I would also be able to avoid using drag-lifts which I hated. Hans had also provided me with all the equipment I needed - skis, boots, goggles, jacket and waterproof trousers - begged and borrowed in the right sizes from various friends.

"There's no point in buying all this stuff," he said, "until you're sure you're going to ski regularly. You might decide you hate it."

It was a beautifully clear winter's morning and from high up on the *Mutterer Alm* I could see right down into the valley, across the town and over to the *Nordkette* range directly opposite. By taking my bearings from the scar on the mountainside made by the tracks of the *Hungerburg* funicular railway, I could virtually pick out the street where I lived. It completed the panoramic view I'd seen half of on my trip up the *Hungerburg* with Mike.

Hans patiently showed me how to put my feet on the skis, pressing down on the little metal knob under my heel so that the bindings clicked into place. Then he knelt down, took out a small screwdriver and adjusted something on the side of my ski.

"I'm making your bindings fairly loose," he explained, "so that they

171

break open with any sharp movement. It'll probably be annoying because your skis will sometimes come off when you don't want them to, but until you know what you're doing it's safer that way. It's better to lose your skis than break a leg."

He then tied a small red cord round each ankle and attached it to the ski.

"If your skis do come off the cord will stop them sliding all the way down the mountain on their own. Not only would that leave you stranded in the snow but it could also kill someone further down the slope. People have been impaled on runaway skis before now."

Satisfied that I was ready, he quickly put on his own skis and tied the cords.

I noticed he didn't adjust his own bindings.

"What about your bindings?" I asked him. "How are they set?"

"Very tight. I sometimes make sharp movements deliberately at high speed and then it's actually dangerous to lose your skis. And, of course, when I was skiing slalom competitions, I used to have them virtually locked. The last thing you want on a sharp slalom turn in a competition is for your skis to come flying off."

Slowly we made our way across the snow to the plateau area at the top of the slope. It was three years since I'd done any skiing, and then only for a few days on my own, self taught, in a tiny French resort, and the skis felt heavy and awkward. My natural instinct was to try and walk, lifting my feet, but this was impossible and I was forced instead to push myself along with my poles inch by inch. I could see Hans ahead of me, legs together, skis parallel, gliding along effortlessly, experience and confidence showing in every movement. At the top of the slope he stopped and waited for me to catch him up.

"OK," he said, "before we start going down, I want you to do a simple exercise. Watch me."

Lightly, he crouched down and dropped back until he was sitting on his skis, then, in one flowing movement, he used his ski poles to push himself upright.

"See. It's easy. Now you try it."

I did and it wasn't. It was impossible. For a start, my legs weren't supple enough for me to ease myself down slowly and it was a case of an inelegant crouch followed by a controlled crash onto my backside. Then once in a sitting position any pressure on my poles forced the skis to slide forward causing me to crash back down again. Hans left me to it for a while, watching me slipping and sliding and bumping for a full five minutes before coming to my rescue and standing with his own skis across the ends of mine to stop them moving forward.

"Right. Now try it again."

For the next fifteen minutes he put me through the same routine over and over again - sit, push, stand, sit, push, stand - until in the end I thought I was going to be crippled for life. My knees, ankles and shoulders felt like somebody had been beating them with a sledgehammer and I was rapidly going off the whole idea of skiing. In the end, I got irritated.

"Look, Hans, what is the point of all this?" I asked bolshily. "I mean what's it got to do with skiing? If I fall over on the slope I can just lie against the gradient and push myself up. It's a waste of time."

"It is not a waste of time. For a start, it loosens up the muscles you need for skiing, including all the ones you probably haven't used for years. For another thing, it warms you up and lessens the risk of cold muscle damage. I bet you're not feeling the cold are you?"

He was right, I wasn't. The sweat was pouring off me.

"But most importantly of all," he continued," if you ever want to be any kind of real skier, as opposed to a once-a-year amateur, you'll need to be able to do simple things like adjust your bindings without having to take your bloody skis off. OK?" He looked at me belligerently.

I nodded, chastened.

"Next time we come up here we'll practice that until you can stand up without me holding your skis for you. But we'll leave it for today and get on with some skiing."

We went over to where the terrain began to slope more steeply and become the piste and Hans began to explain about the snow-plough, the basic position for controlling one's descent and stopping. As usual, I wanted to run before I could walk and prove that I wasn't a complete beginner.

"It's alright, Hans," I interrupted him, "I know about the snow-plough. I skied in France, remember?"

Hans heaved a deep sigh.

"Go on then," he said with a longsuffering look, "show me what you can do."

Well I had skied before and I had just about mastered the snow-plough but three years is a long time and any skill I might have acquired was lying very dormant. No sooner had I started to move than my skis crossed in front of me and locked together. I slid forwards totally out of control until finally I toppled over and bounced several feet down the mountainside on my back before coming to rest in an ungainly heap. Hans followed and glided to a graceful stop beside me. He looked down at my prostrate form and shook his head sorrowfully.

"That may be how they ski in France," he said, "but in Austria we do it on our feet. I suggest you forget anything you may or may not have learned before, listen to me and do as I tell you."

It was a rotten morning. Hans was a very hard, very strict taskmaster and conducted his training with almost military discipline. He made me perform each manoeuvre over and over again, correcting each tiny mistake until he was satisfied that I was doing it as well as I possibly could. By midday, we had still only got as far as the first rest point on the slope and I had seen the same people passing us time and time again as they completed the run and went back up for another go. In addition my back, posterior and thighs were just a mass of bruises where I'd fallen over with monotonous regularity. I was beginning to wish I'd never mentioned skiing to Hans.

We stopped and had lunch in the small restaurant at the rest point but I was too miserable to enjoy it much. I was sullen and unresponsive to Hans because I felt he was being too hard on me, making it too much like work to be enjoyable. It didn't occur to me at the time but Hans was a professional and I was being given free tuition that other people paid several hundred schillings an hour for, provided of course he felt like teaching them. Yet here was I acting like a spoilt child. It was gross ingratitude and I felt very guilty when I thought back on it later.

After lunch things began to improve. Hans continued with the coaching, teaching me to traverse the slope instead of just heading straight down, or, in my case, falling straight down.

"After all," he explained, "it's not a race. It takes a long while to come back up to the top and you can waste an awful lot of your day on lifts if you just hurtle down the slope as fast as you can. You need to use the slope, crossing it from side to side to increase the distance."

We practised this for another hour or so and the Hans decided we'd had enough for one day.

"We've got about half the length of this slope left to play with," he said, "so we're going to finish with a straight run down. I just want you to follow me, turning where I turn and remembering what I've shown you this morning. I'll pick out the easiest route and you just keep in my tracks. OK?"

It was on the final run down that I at last remembered why I'd chosen to come to Innsbruck in the first place. I got a taste once again of the exhilaration I'd first felt in the French Alps three years before. There was something about the freedom of skiing, the cold wind stinging your face, the gentle shush of your skis on the snow, the exciting sense of being in control of your own body that no other sport could match. I was still far from being even a competent skier and I fell three times en route, but at least I knew now why I wanted to ski well and why it was worth putting up with the hard training necessary to make it possible. By the time I reached the bottom, I wasn't miserable any longer. I felt I'd actually achieved something that day apart from the world record for the most bruises on one body.

As we packed our skis back on the roof rack of Hans' car and prepared to go home he stopped for a moment and looked thoughtful before turning to me.

"You know, where we go from here is really up to you now. I've taught you the basics of skiing and we can leave it there if you want to. You know enough to have some fun on the slopes while you're here in Austria. On the other hand, I could make you into a real skier if you wanted. I don't mean competition class or anything like that but good enough to hold your own in most company. But that, unfortunately, would take a lot of work and most of the time it wouldn't be as much fun as just playing around by yourself." He smiled. "I know you didn't really enjoy it much today so it's up to you really."

I didn't need to give it much consideration. I knew now what I wanted.

"I want to learn to ski well," I told him. "I'd be stupid to pass up the opportunity while I'm here. That's if you're willing to put up with me."

Hans laughed.

"Of course I am. But you're going to have to work at it. For a start, you'd better come up here on your days off and practise and I'll arrange to come up and coach you whenever I can. Once you've mastered this slope, which shouldn't take very long, we can move further afield and do some real skiing. We might even try the Olympic slopes if you do well enough."

It sounded great. If I could master skiing and learn to speak German reasonably well by the time I'd finished in Austria, then the year would have been well worthwhile whatever else happened.

"There is one thing, though," said Hans as we got in the car.

"What's that?"

If you thought today was rough, wait until we really get going. I'll make you wish you'd stayed in England."

He grinned broadly, started the car and drove off.

On Tuesday at school Reiner came and found me during the first break.

"Right, renegade, you've got a chance to redeem yourself tonight."

"What do you mean 'redeem myself'?"

"Make up for your appalling treachery last week, that's what I mean."

Reiner had made great mileage out of my treachery, as he called it, after the football match. Hardly a day had gone by without some reference to language assistants who didn't know their place or foreigners devoid of any notion of loyalty. I suspected that this was his way of laughing off his embarrassment at what had happened that evening.

"I'm playing volleyball tonight," I said cautiously.

"No volleyball tonight, I'm afraid. Tonight is *Kollegenabend*."

"What's *Kollegenabend*?"

"Well every couple of months or so, in the interests of staff unity, the Headmaster organises a get-together at a local pub. He normally gives a quick pep-talk and then hands over to a member of staff who provides a scintillating evening's entertainment, you know, a talk on 'My stamp collection' or 'Folk dancing in Lithuania' something like that. This evening's offering is 'My holiday among the Greek ruins' by Frau Henzel."

"Sounds like an evening to be missed at all costs."

"Oh it is. Most definitely. And since it is completely voluntary the vast majority will go out of their way to miss it. Unfortunately, that doesn't include me or indeed you if you know what's good for you."

"Why you and me particularly?"

"Well it's an unwritten rule that senior members of staff and Heads of Department make damn sure they attend unless they've got a bloody good excuse not to. They're expected to show a lead to the less dedicated members of staff and demonstrate their loyalty to the Headmaster."

"Oh I get it. And I'm so well thought of that I've been reclassified as a senior member of staff?"

"Not exactly, no. More the exact opposite really. Most of the English staff won't be seen dead there but your junior enough for me to put the finger on you. After all I'm the one who drew up that terribly nice timetable. It would be a real pity if I had to change it due to unforeseen circumstances."

I didn't take this threat seriously for a moment. I knew Reiner well enough by now to know he wasn't that petty. This was his way of asking me to help him out by going, presumably to please the Headmaster. I had no reason not to go anyway if volleyball was cancelled.

"That sounds disturbingly like moral blackmail," I said, feigning indignation.

"No, no, not at all," replied Reiner, "there's nothing moral about it. It's blackmail pure and simple."

"I suppose I'd better be there then."

"Funny, I thought you might say that. I'd always suspected you were a secret Greek ruin fancier. It starts at eight in the *Weisse Hirsch*. No need to book a table, we're not expecting a crowd."

"How long will it drag on?"

"Not more than a couple of hours, I shouldn't think. But don't make any plans. I'll be needing a drinking companion afterwards to help me wash away the memory and guess who's also volunteered for that?"

I couldn't help but admire the sheer audacity of the man.

"Alright," I agreed, "I'll see you at eight."

I arrived at the inn dead on eight o'clock and bumped into Suzi, the young first-year probationary teacher from the English department, in the doorway.

"Hello," I said, "you decided to come too, did you?"

"Oh, yes," she said cheerfully, "Reiner said it would be a good opportunity to get to know everybody a bit better in an informal atmosphere. Apparently, it's normally an interesting and enjoyable evening."

I decided I'd better not tell her what Reiner had said to me. He'd obviously missed his vocation. He should have been a diplomat. Instead I just said:

"So I hear. Shall we go in?"

The school had taken a private room upstairs for the evening and when we entered two waiters were setting up a white projector screen at the front while a third wandered around taking orders for drinks. It was quite a good turn-out, much to my surprise, and there were getting on for fifty people grouped around tables strategically placed to give a good view of the screen. As Reiner had feared, most of the English department were conspicuous by their absence. Only Else Grindl and Dr. Bürger had made the effort. I also noticed without surprise that most of my football and volleyball playing colleagues had also failed to turn up. Those present were mainly either very senior members of staff or very new ones. The rest presumably had mixed reasons for being there ranging from wanting an evening away from the wife to wanting to make a good impression on the Headmaster.

Suzi went off and joined a group of other first-year teachers at a table while I looked around for a place to sit. Eventually, I noticed Reiner waving at me from a crowded table in the middle of the room. There was an empty seat next to him which I guessed he had kept for me.

"Hi, boss," I said "your loyal servant has arrived."

178

"Well done," he answered, "thanks for making it. Sit down and I'll get you a drink."

It seemed to me that, far from being there against his will, Reiner was actually enjoying himself. He seemed to be the focus of attention at the table and was revelling in playing the life and soul of the party. He was capable of great humour in English but in his own earthy, Tyrolean dialect he was a master, producing a continuous stream of clever puns, witty remarks and acerbic comments which had his audience in fits. Unfortunately, I had never managed to get used to Reiner's German and after a number of abortive attempts to hold a conversation at the beginning of my stay, we had quickly realised that it was a waste of time and always spoke in English to each other. Now I was starting to regret it since I could only understand one word in five and was missing all the jokes. All I could do was just laugh when everyone else did and pretend I was following it all.

When he was sure that everyone who was going to come had arrived, the Headmaster stood up and waited for silence. Slowly the conversations came to an end and the audience gave him their attention and waited for the evening's entertainment to begin.

"My dear colleagues," said the Headmaster, "thank you for being here this evening. It is always a pleasure to see so many of you gathered together like this and I am grateful that you have been willing to spare precious time away from your families to attend. It is particularly gratifying to see so many of our newer members of staff here tonight."

I caught Reiner's eye at this point and he smiled ironically.

"Let me begin by briefly reviewing the academic year so far."

For five minutes or so the Headmaster talked about what had happened during the term and outlined the aims of the school for the rest of the year. He welcomed all the new members of staff by name, including me, and gave a brief obituary for a retired teacher who had recently died.

"And now," he said finally, duty done, "without further ado, let me hand over to Irma Henzel who will give us, what I'm sure will be a most edifying talk, on Classical Greece. Irma."

Unfortunately there was a slight hiatus at this point. Frau Henzel, a small, mousy, middle-aged lady who taught French and philosophy, was still at the back of the room struggling to load a carousel of slides into the projector. We all waited patiently, pretending not to hear the rattling and banging which were growing louder and louder as she got more and more agitated.

"If she goes on like that much longer," whispered Reiner to me, "we'll have more than just Greek ruins to look at."

Eventually there was a loud click followed by an audible sigh of relief from Frau Henzel and she announced proudly:

"Right. I think I'm ready now. I'll just come to the front and then could someone dim the lights for me?"

She went forward holding a remote control device attached to a long cable. This impeded her progress somewhat and twice she was held up for several moments when the cable tangled itself round a chair but at last she arrived at the front and sat down on a stool to the right of the large screen. Obligingly the Headmaster moved to the back of the room and turned off all the lights. There was another moment of silence before she stood up again.

"Er..um..actually," she said, "could I have the lights back on again? I'd forgotten about my introduction thing."

The Headmaster walked back to the wall and switched on the lights before returning to his seat again. It was hardly worth it.

"So," said Frau Henzel, "tonight I am going to show you the slides taken by my husband and myself on our trip last year to Greece. The talk is entitled 'The Ruins of Greece'. Thank you Headmaster.

Once again the long-suffering Headmaster walked all the way back and turned off the lights. But this time he waited until the first slide was up on the screen before going back to his seat. He wasn't going to be caught out again.

The first slide showed a fat, middle-aged man, presumably Herr Henzel, posing self-consciously, suitcase in hand, in front of their house. This was followed by a shot of Frau Henzel waving goodbye to relatives as she climbed into a car and then a very blurred picture of some houses shot through the window of a moving vehicle. In the next slide, we had arrived at Innsbruck main station and, in the one after that, Herr Henzel was standing pointing at a train - the train that would take them to Greece. And that's how it continued, every step of the journey painstakingly recorded in minute detail.

"Oh God," whispered Reiner after five minutes of this, "we're going to get a blow by blow account of the whole holiday. At this rate, it'd be quicker to go to Greece ourselves and see the bloody ruins."

After a further ten minutes, I was beginning to think he was right. There had already been some thirty slides and we still hadn't got past their arrival at the hotel on the first day in Greece. Admittedly, we had seen lots of nice photographs of Herr Henzel eating breakfast on the train and Frau Henzel buying sandwiches from mobile shops en route not to mention blurred views of the Italian countryside and slides of passport officers in national uniforms posing stiffly for the camera, but there had been precious little to excite fans of classical Greek architecture. Nobody seemed particularly bothered, though. Very few, if any, of the people present were there out of love for ancient Greek monuments. The only worry they might have had was that expressed by someone on my table.

"If she takes this long over the preamble God alone knows how long she'll spend on the main bit. We could be here all night."

We needn't have worried, however. The slides of the Greek ruins, when they finally arrived, were behind us in no time at all and they, like everything else, served merely as a backdrop against which the chief protagonists could be shown enjoying their holiday. After a few quick views of Herr Henzel standing in front of the Parthenon and his good lady wife seated on bits of what remained of this or that temple, we returned to out-of-focus shots of the hotel they were staying in and one or other of them enjoying a drink outside a cafe. Very soon it was back to the train for the long journey home, more views of the Italian countryside and, with a final climactic shot of Innsbruck station in all its glory, the edifying talk was brought to a close.

There was loud applause from the audience and a few good-natured calls of 'bravo' and 'well done'. The Headmaster turned the lights back on revealing a blushing, delighted Frau Henzel fiddling nervously with the little box on her hands. He came forward to join her at the front and raised his hands for silence. When the applause had died away, he addressed the audience.

"Well I'm sure you all join with me in thanking Irma for that most interesting presentation. I'm confident I speak for everyone when I say it was a most enjoyable and most entertaining look at the er.. Greek ruins. I'd like to thank all of you for coming this evening and giving me your support. The next *Kollegenabend* will be in January and let us all make an effort to persuade more of our colleagues to attend next time. And now, as it's getting late and many of you have families to get back to, I'll draw this meeting to a close. Thank you colleagues."

There was a further outbreak of clapping and then the buzz of conversation rose again punctuated by the scraping of chairs and calls to the waiter for bills to be brought. Reiner paid his bill and mine and got up.

"Come on," he said, "let's get out of here and go and get a drink somewhere."

We ended up in a bar down by the river. Reiner, as usual drank prodigiously and I had tremendous difficulty keeping up with him. He wouldn't hear of me dropping out of a round or having a small beer instead of a large one and by the end of the evening I had them lined up on the table.

"Bloody hell, you're slow," he said, looking at his watch. "We need to leave here soon if we're going to make it into school tomorrow. Come on, I'll give you a hand to shift these."

We both drank two large beers in quick succession, paid the bill and left to find Reiner's car. By the time we reached it, I was beginning to feel very uncomfortable. My bladder had become something of a standing joke with Mike and two large beers thrown down at that speed were guaranteed to cause problems. I was too shy to say anything to Reiner, though, and I just hoped I could hang on until he got me home.

It was a forlorn hope. After a few minutes rocking around in the car the pressure was becoming unbearable. I had no choice.

"Reiner," I asked him, "is there anywhere we can stop? I'm bursting and I can't wait."

"Yes, I could do with a pee, as it happens. Just hang on and I'll find somewhere."

He swung the car round into the next right-hand turning, zigzagged round a series of small side roads and drew up by an area of park at the back of the Palace Gardens.

"We can pop in here," he said, "and find a convenient tree. There won't be anyone about at this time of night. We'll have to climb the gate, though. I suspect it's probably locked."

I was in agony by this time. Even getting out of the car and walking were painful and climbing the gate was sheer purgatory. But at last I made it and went thankfully behind the nearest tree. As I began to unleash the flood and the sweet feeling of relief flowed through me, Nature decided to join in too and the first flakes of snow started to fall in the town. In no time at all, they were swirling down in thick white clouds, settling as they landed.

"I think you'd better hurry up," shouted Reiner, from behind an adjacent tree."

"Why?" I called back.

"Because it's beginning to snow quite heavily and the temperature's dropping."

He finished what he was doing and came towards my tree. I could see him grinning. "It wouldn't look good, you know, the Head of the English department and his English assistant both found in a park in the middle of the night with frost-bitten penises. Nobody would ever believe we were just here to water the plants."

Chapter Seventeen

It continued snowing heavily throughout the night and when I woke the next morning and looked out of the window the whole face of the street had changed. Road and pavement, grass and concrete had all disappeared, buried under a thick blanket of clean, white snow. Houses were snow-capped like mountains, trees had turned white and the cars parked overnight in the road were now just huge white blobs on the landscape. It was all quite magical and I was delighted it had happened at last.

I'd always liked the snow, especially before Christmas and, since today was the first of December, the timing was impeccable. It gave me a warm glow inside looking out at the steadily falling snow and realizing that in three weeks I would be back in England again, reunited with my family for Christmas. Both Mike and I had had invitations to stay with people in Innsbruck over the holiday but we had decided it would do us good to go home for a couple of weeks. The money was no problem and it would give us time to get into perspective everything that had happened so far. Living abroad like this was somehow unreal and we both felt that we would only appreciate it properly, looking back on it from a distance. We had already made most of the arrangements, choosing the long train journey through Germany and Belgium in preference to a flight from Munich. Neither of us liked flying and we both wanted a period of adjustment before returning to England. We'd had to get permission from our schools to take an extra day off work since term didn't finish until the 23rd. We naturally wanted to get home before Christmas Eve which meant leaving on the afternoon of the 22nd. For me, it would be a twenty-six hour journey and for Mike slightly less since he lived near Dover. Permission had been granted without hesitation.

I was in a cheerful mood throughout the morning at school and, reflecting my preoccupation of the moment, I decided to talk about Christmas in all of my conversation classes. It turned out to be quite an eye-opener for me. As I talked to the various classes it became clear that Christmas in Austria was very different to the one I was used to at home. For a start, the main event took place on Christmas Eve not Christmas Day as in England, and the bringer of gifts was the Baby Jesus, *Das Kristkind*, rather than Father Christmas. On the night of the 24th the children were kept occupied elsewhere while, behind closed doors, their presents were laid out around the tree. They were then allowed into the room to see their gifts before being taken off to midnight mass with their parents. St. Nicholas had his day some weeks before on the sixth of December and for the Austrians this marked the real beginning of the Christmas season. By tradition, on this day, the children were given little models of St. Nicholas or the Devil made out of papier-mâché or coloured pipe-cleaners accompanied by a selection of nuts, fruits and seasonal sweetmeats. Since the sixth fell on a Monday this year most people would celebrate on the Sunday, I was told. Both the big days were preceded by a traditional market. In the weeks before Christmas Eve there was the *Kristkindmarkt* peddling a mixture of traditional religious and secular items such as candles, nativity figures, tree decorations and yuletide cakes and biscuits. And leading up to St. Nicholas' day, there was normally a smaller market selling bits and pieces like devils' tails, little wooden two-pronged forks and coloured pipe-cleaners to make the figures along with nuts, dried fruits and little heart shaped biscuits. By tradition the market always began on December the first, which was today, in the main square of the Old Town. I could hardly wait until lunchtime to go and see it.

I met Mike at the usual place.

"Look at that," he said. "Isn't it fantastic?"

The whole square in front of the *Goldenes Dachl* had been transformed, first by the snow and then by the addition of an enormous Christmas tree and several rows of old-fashioned market stalls. Men on ladders were still threading lights among the branches of the tree but the market was already in full swing. In addition to the stalls selling goods, there was a man seated beside a glowing brazier selling hot chestnuts and the inevitable sausage seller tending grills and pans of sizzling and boiling sausages. The square was thronged with people, busily buying what they needed for Sunday and excited children ran from stall to stall staring wide-eyed at the goods on display, scarcely daring to believe that Christmas was at last nearly here again.

"What's it for, though?" Mike asked. "It's a bit early for Christmas, isn't it?"

I explained briefly what I had picked up from my pupils that morning.

"Ah, I see," he said. "Well that explains something else as well then. I saw Maurice this morning and we've all been invited to Helga's on Sunday evening to eat goulash."

"Is goulash part of the tradition then?" I asked.

"Not a clue. You're the expert."

"Well I doubt it somehow. It's not exactly dripping with religious significance, is it, goulash?"

"No I suppose not."

Mike was still staring raptly at the scene in the square.

"I really like this," he said. "It makes me feel quite Christmassy. Why don't we come back here after lunch and have our coffee and cake in the square for a change? We can watch it all while we're eating and then have a good look round afterwards."

"Ok. Why not?"

We began to walk off towards the *Mensa* but Mike turned round again for a moment and surveyed the scene in the square.

"I'll tell you something," he said. "They certainly know how to do things in style the Austrians, don't they?"

On Sunday, just as I was sitting down to a very late breakfast in my room, there was a knock at the door.

"Come in," I called, "it's open."

"I can't," came Ingrid's voice through the door, "my hands are full. You'll have to open it for me."

I got up and opened the door to find Ingrid standing there with a wooden bread board in her hands. On the board stood a little model of a red devil surrounded by nuts, dried figs and several small tangerines.

"This is for you. Happy St. Nicholas day!"

This came as a complete surprise and I was really touched.

"That's wonderful, Ingrid," I said. "I didn't expect even to see one of these. I thought they were only given to children."

"Well, they can be given to any member of the family really, and you're virtually part of the family now, aren't you? I gave one to Herbie, too, but then he actually is more like one of my children. I sometimes wonder what he'd do without me."

"We all wonder what we'd do without you," I said and kissed her on the cheek. "Thanks for the present. It was a lovely thought."

"Not at all. I'm glad you're pleased. You're invited to dinner tonight as well if you can make it."

"I can't unfortunately. I've already been invited to eat goulash with some friends."

"Oh well then, not to worry." She smiled mischievously. "But don't eat all those figs today, will you? Could be very nasty on top of goulash." She rubbed her stomach, laughing. "If you know what I mean?"

At eight o'clock Mike and I arrived at Helga's flat and rang the bell. It was Lisa who opened the door.

"Hello," she said, "come on in."

We stomped the snow off our shoes, brushed off our overcoats and followed her inside. It was good to get into the warm again. It was freezing outside.

"Here let me take your coats. The others are in the sitting-room and Helga's preparing dinner in the kitchen. It could be some time judging by the noise and the swearing."

We handed over our coats and went into the sitting room where Chantal and Maurice were sipping drinks. Lisa, having offloaded our coats, bustled in behind us, determined to fulfil her role as co-hostess.

"Right," she said, "what would you like to drink? There's beer, whisky and I think we've got some Campari somewhere."

"Whisky for me please," said Mike.

"And for me, too," I agreed.

Lisa busied herself pouring the drinks while we sat down with the others.

"Recovered from your bruises yet," Mike said to Chantal.

She pouted and rubbed her shoulder.

"No I haven't. You children with your silly snowballs. I think I'll be marked for life."

The previous evening the four of us had gone for dinner in the Old Town. After a meal in one of the restaurants around the square we had joined the groups of people wandering around the now brightly-lit Christmas tree and making their final purchases from the market stalls. Like children, caught up in the excitement, we had begun to play around in the snow, grabbing handfuls and throwing them gently at each other. Before long a full scale war had broken out, England versus France, with snowballs flying harder and harder and faster and faster across the square. Chantal had proved herself a more deadly enemy than Maurice and, as a consequence, she had taken the main brunt of our attack. It had all been in fun and nobody had really been hurt but Chantal had complained with mock indignation all the way home about her bruises.

"I didn't notice you refusing to join in the silly game last night," I said. "You threw more snowballs than the rest of us put together."

"Ah, but that was a matter of honour," she answered pompously. "I was defending my country - a magnificent female warrior like a modern-day Joan of Arc."

"Right then," said Mike, "next time we won't bother with the snowballs. We'll just tie you to the Christmas tree and set fire to you."

Chantal's squeal of protest was cut short by the appearance of Helga from the kitchen sporting an apron bearing a large Snoopy cartoon.

"Hello my children," she said gaily," I hope you're all starving. There's enough goulash out there to feed an army."

"And if you don't finish it tonight," said Lisa, "guess who's going to have to live on it for the next week?"

"What kind of goulash is it?" Mike asked.

"Pork," replied Helga.

"Oh dear. That could be a problem."

"Why?"

"Well, Iain's Jewish, you see. He's not allowed to eat pork."

"Oh, no," Helga cried with real dismay. "I didn't know. What on earth are we going to do?"

Then she noticed Mike laughing and realized we were pulling

her leg.

"Oh really! I suppose that's English humour is it? Well, you'd better be careful Mr. English funny man or there'll be a good deal more than pork in your goulash."

With a fine show of indignance she turned on her heel and flounced back into the kitchen.

The meal, when it was finally served, was excellent, far better than anything I'd eaten in the *Mensa* or the restaurants, and Lisa's fears about a pork goulash diet for the next week proved unfounded. As we sat over our coffee, I noticed Helga signal surreptitiously to Lisa and they both stood up.

"Would you excuse us for a moment?" Helga asked. "We're just going to bring in the drinks in case anybody wants something."

Together they left the dining-room and disappeared in the direction of Helga's bedroom.

"That's a funny place to keep the drinks," said Maurice suspiciously. "What are they up to?"

We all strained to listen to what was going on but all we could hear was a whispered conversation and the sound of cupboard doors being opened and closed. After several minutes, we were all bursting with curiosity, eager to know what mischief they were planning between them. Eventually, the whispering stopped and we heard the bedroom door opening as our hostesses prepared to rejoin us. They appeared in the doorway holding a tray covered with a white cloth and gently walked over and placed it on the table. Then, with due ceremony. Helga whipped off the cloth, like a magician performing his show-stopping final trick and together they chorused:

"Happy St. Nicholas day!"

On the tray stood four little devils modelled with great skill out of papier-mâché and carefully painted red and black. Next to each was a small plastic bag containing the now familiar selection of nuts and fruit.

"There's one each," said Helga proudly. "It's a tradition here in Austria."

"Yes," said Lisa, "we were sure you would never have seen anything like this before."

Mike looked at me and smiled quietly but neither of us said a word. We weren't going to spoil their fun.

Chapter Eighteen

"That's all agreed then, is it?" asked Chantal, a picture of brisk efficiency. "I'll get four tickets and then you can pay me back afterwards. I don't think they'll cost all that much."

"No problem," replied Mike. "What time's it start?"

"Oh, let's aim to get there about nine, give it a chance to warm up."

The 'it' in question was a Christmas party up in the Romance Language faculty at the University, grandly entitled *Romanistisches Fest*, and scheduled for the next evening. Chantal had found out about it by chance on a visit to the faculty library that morning and had sought out the three of us in the *Mensa* to see if we wanted to go along. Mike and I jumped at the idea. With just over a week to go before returning home for Christmas, we were in the right mood for a bit of frivolous entertainment. Maurice was less enthusiastic, not being over keen on dancing and loud music, but he allowed himself to be persuaded in the end, especially as Chantal was going home in a few days time. With typical good fortune, and no doubt because she was female, she had been given three days off by her school to allow her to travel home at the weekend. She was intending to leave early Saturday morning while Mike and I would have to wait until the following Wednesday before starting the long trek home. Maurice, fanatical in his desire to remain immersed in German for as long as possible, was staying in Innsbruck and celebrating Christmas with the family he lived with.

We finalised the arrangements with Chantal and then put our minds to deciding what we were going to do with the afternoon. Chantal was not normally in the habit of eating in the *Mensa* at lunchtimes. She served two schools outside Innsbruck and ate locally with the other teachers when she was teaching and cooked for herself at home when she wasn't. It seemed a pity not to make the most of her company on the one occasion when we had it.

"Well I've still got piles of Christmas shopping to do," she said. "I haven't brought any presents at all yet. But I don't suppose shopping is really your idea of fun, is it?"

Mike and I looked at each other with superior smiles.

"You obviously don't know us very well at all," he said. "You're looking at two world-class shoppers here."

"Olympic champions," I agreed. "What we don't know about the shops in Innsbruck you could write on the back of a very small 'special offer' coupon."

Chantal laughed.

"Oh forgive my ignorance," she said. "I wasn't aware I was in the presence of greatness." She turned to Maurice. "What about you. Are you a gold-medallist too?"

"No, just an also-ran, I'm happy to say. But I haven't done any Christmas shopping either so today's as good a day as any. We should go to the *Kristkindmarkt*, though, rather than the shops."

The *Kristkindmarkt* had now taken the place of the St. Nicholas Day market in the town square.

"OK then," said Chantal, "that settles it. But I want a coffee and a cake first to build up my strength. I hate Christmas shopping."

The snow had fallen heavily this year, even by Innsbruck's standards, and in and around the Old Town, where cars were banned, it was piled high on the ground. Although the authorities did a sterling job of keeping the roads clear and safe, pedestrian areas took second place and, with so much snow falling all the time, these were never fully cleared. In the end, I'd even gone so far as to buy a pair of wellington boots because I was fed up with wandering around all day with wet feet and soggy trouser bottoms. For me this was a tremendously extravagant purchase since shoes were very expensive in Austria and my father actually ran a small shoe shop back in England. Two more weeks and I could have had a pair for nothing. But after a lot of thought, personal comfort proved the victor over parsimony in the end and I'd parted with the necessary small fortune.

The *Kristkindmarkt* was a far grander affair than the earlier market. It stretched right down into the narrow streets of the Old Town and had everything from tree decorations to liqueur chocolates, and well-made, tasteful gifts to cheap, shoddy rubbish. Chantal, Mike and I were desperate to take part of Austria back home with us - not souvenirs because that would have made us seem like tourists - but ordinary, simple, everyday things that the Austrians themselves might buy. It was as if, subconsciously, we wanted to demonstrate that we were not just visiting Austria but actually lived there, belonged there. So we wandered around buying the mundane items such as Christmas cards and tree decorations, calendars and candles and the inevitable *Lebkuchen* and *Stollen* - the little biscuits and fruit loaves traditionally eaten at Christmas. Beyond that Mike and I had very little interest in the stalls selling gifts. During the long period without money, window-shopping for Christmas presents had been another game we'd played as a substitute for not being able to buy anything and in the weeks after the first pay-day we had systematically done the rounds of the shops collecting up all the items we'd settled on. However, neither of us had any objection to watching Chantal and Maurice going through the painful process and we followed them round offering helpful and, as often as not, unhelpful advice on what to buy.

The next evening at nine o'clock we gathered outside the Romance Language faculty at the university. It looked like they'd had little difficulty in selling the tickets. A continuous stream of people was passing through the makeshift turnstile in the entrance to the building and the sound of music, shouting and laughter coming from inside showed the party was already in full swing.

"Right, here you are then," said Chantal, handing round the tickets. "They were only thirty schillings each and that includes a free drink when you go in, so I don't think that's too bad."

"Pretty reasonable for an evening out," said Mike, giving her thirty schillings in return.

"It sounds like there's a war going on in there," moaned Maurice. "Do they always have to have the music so loud?"

"Oh, you're such a wet blanket," said Chantal. "Where's your spirit of adventure, your get up and go?" She smiled mischievously at Mike and me. "You're supposed to be French, man, not English."

"Alright," I put in, "when you've quite finished trying to create racial conflict I'll have my ticket please. And any more remarks like that and Mike and I will refuse to dance with you and keep our natural sense of rhythm and superb physical control to ourselves."

"And dance with each other," added Mike.

She handed over my ticket, giggling, and we went to join the party.

Inside it looked like Maurice had been right after all and there really was a war going on. The air was filled with smoke, people were milling around in groups shouting to each other to make themselves heard and the incessant beat of the drums from the small band up on the stage, coupled with the stomping and jumping up and down of the dancers made the whole room shake. The place was packed out and getting over to the long trestle table in one corner which served as a makeshift bar was no easy matter. When we finally reached it, I had my doubts whether the effort had really been worthwhile. All that was on offer was a lethal looking red liquid with slices of fruit floating in it.

"What is it?" Mike asked the student acting as barman.

"It's sangria," he replied cautiously, "a kind of punch made out of red wine and things."

Mike and I looked at each other dubiously. We'd been to student parties before.

"I'm not too worried about the red wine part of it," said Mike, "it's the 'things' which bother me. Could you be a little more specific?"

Unfortunately, he wasn't able to enlighten us any more.

"Well, actually, I didn't make it but I'm sure there's only a bit of fruit juice in there."

Chantal, as usual, was braver than the rest of us.

"Look instead of just standing here talking about it, why don't we drink some instead. The first one's free anyway. What have we got to lose?"

"Oh nothing much," said Mike. "Teeth, taste buds, stomach lining, that sort of thing. Nothing crucial."

"Oh, come on."

Exasperated, she exchanged her ticket for a white paper cup of the brew and, with a fine show of bravado, took a hefty swig. It proved to be an unwise move. Her face registered shock and she gasped out loud before convulsing in a fit of coughing. But she wasn't going to be beaten. When the coughs subsided and she'd wiped the tears from her eyes she announced hoarsely:

"See, no problem. It's quite good."

Put to shame by Chantal the three of us dutifully handed over our tickets and took our drinks in return. Mike sipped delicately at his.

"Well he was right about the fruit juice," he said, "it's definitely in here. He just forgot to tell us that they'd fermented and distilled it first."

I took a sip. It was about forty percent schnapps.

"We'd better go very easy on this stuff tonight," I said, "or we may well end up doing something we'll regret tomorrow. I for one don't want to be remembered in years to come as the mad Englishman who danced naked around the Christmas tree in the Old Town."

In retrospect, I should have taken better heed of my own warning.

By midnight the party had reached its climax. The dance floor was packed solid with people, the band had turned the amplifiers right up and were hammering out English pop songs with a frenzy that had to be seen to be believed and everywhere there was a sea of happy, laughing faces basking in the end of term atmosphere. I felt good, really good. I had drunk rather a lot of the sangria and it had left me feeling bright and lively and relatively uninhibited. I had lost the others fairly early on and I had spent the last couple of hours wandering among the various groups, picking out here and there people I recognised and joining in their conversations. The sangria had done wonders for my German and I was on good form. So much so that twice, by avoiding long and difficult sentences and keeping it simple, I had been taken for a southern German, much to my delight. Boosted by these minor successes and buoyed up by the sangria I was now looking around for someone to dance with. Normally very conscious of my limitations in that area, and totally inhibited as a consequence, I tended to avoid dancing like the plague. But tonight was different. If I could pass for a German, I could dance as well. By sheer chance, before I could proposition some complete stranger, I bumped into Chantal. I could tell from her bright shining eyes and flushed cheeks that she'd also taken a liking to the sangria.

"Hi," she said, "isn't it a great party?"

"It sure is. Hey, come and have a dance with me. I'm fed up with talking above all this noise."

"OK. Push a way through and I'll follow you."

We battled our way through the crowds and managed to find a tiny area of the dance floor to stand on. It was too packed to dance properly so we just held onto each other and moved as much as we could in time to the music. The band had struck up a rousing Spanish song, simple but loud and rhythmic and we were soon swept up in the general bouncing up and down, the laughing and the shouting. Egged on by success the band continued the trend of loud, bouncy songs and we remained there on the dance floor, totally caught up in the atmosphere, hugging each other, giggling and laughing like children, moving wildly to the music. And when the pace slowed down and the band began to play a soft romantic song and the lights dimmed even more, it seemed only natural that we stay there, swaying gently with the music, holding each other close.

It was the first time I'd held a girl since the summer in England and it felt good. Chantal was warm and soft in my arms and despite the small warning bell in the back of my mind, I let myself give in to the pleasure of it, held her tighter, pulled her closer. She responded and very soon, almost without realising it, lost in the music and the warmth and the softness, I kissed her.

We remained there, locked together, for what seemed like hours, oblivious to the changes in tempo of the music and the party gradually folding up around us. It was only when a hand was placed on my shoulder and I heard Mike say, "Come on you two lovebirds. We're going on somewhere with some people I've met", that I finally came back to the real world. I felt like I'd just been woken from a beautiful dream and I rubbed my eyes as if I'd been sleeping. Most of the revellers seemed to have gone and the organisers were beginning to tidy up where they could.

"Where are we going?" I asked him. "Everything will be shut by now."

"Apparently there's a small all-night bar down one of the side alleys in the Old Town. These people are members and drink there quite often. Quick come on or they'll go without us."

Still holding Chantal by the hand, I followed him over to where Maurice was standing with three other people I didn't recognise. They were a strange bunch. There was a tall meticulously groomed, ostentatiously well-dressed Frenchman called De Beauvoir who taught language and conversation in the faculty; a small, rather plain girl with her hair in a severe bun called Ewa, who was half French and half Polish and studied English and Philosophy at the University; and an old man whose name I didn't catch who seemed to have decided late in life, after making a fortune in business, to give it all up and take a degree in French. Mike completed the introductions and the old man led us to his large Mercedes parked outside.

"I think we should try to do it in one trip," he suggested, unlocking the doors. "You should all be able to squeeze in with a bit of luck. There's room for two passengers in the front."

It was an inordinately large car and we all got in without too much bother. We weren't too far from the Old Town anyway and in a matter of minutes the old man stopped the car in a dark narrow street to let us pile out into the snow again before driving off to find somewhere suitable to park.

"Where's the bar?" asked Mike.

"This is it here," said De Beauvoir. He pointed at a little wooden door well-hidden in the old stone wall. Above, in letters barely large enough to read, was a notice bearing the legend:

'Bar Napoli - Open 9pm to 6am. Please knock.'

"Not exactly touting for custom, are they?" Mike whispered to me.

De Beauvoir stepped up to the door and rapped on the wooden panels. There was a moment's silence before a window opened in the door and a pair of eyes peered out into the gloom.

"Ah, *Herr Professor* De Beauvoir," said a disembodied voice from somewhere inside, "it's you."

There was the sound of bolts being drawn back and then the door was opened by a young man in a smart dinner suit with a black bow-tie.

"Good evening, sir," he said with a small bow of the head, "how nice to see you again."

"Thank you, Heinrich," replied De Beauvoir with a lordly wave of his hand. "It's very pleasant to be here again. I've brought a few friends along for a nightcap."

"Very good, sir. Is Herr Tapfer not with you tonight?"

"He'll be along in a few moments. He's just parking the car."

"Fine. Well if you would just like to follow me, sir."

Heinrich led us through a narrow hallway, down a flight of stairs and into a small, dimly-lit bar at the bottom. Contrary to appearances from the outside, it was actually a very high-class place with thick pile carpet on the floor and highly polished mahogany tables laid with cocktail titbits. Jazz filtered softly through two large stereo speakers on the wall and all around, seated at tables or standing at the bar were well-dressed, elegant, obviously well-to-do people sipping drinks and chatting quietly to each other. It was clearly a very exclusive place, the domain of Innsbruck's wealthy socialites, which explained the locked door upstairs. I wondered what would have happened if Mike and I had come here on our own. I doubted very much whether we would even have seen the door open. It would have been a quick goodbye through the sliding panel.

Heinrich showed us to a table and then left us in the hands of another smartly dinner-suited waiter who handed us a drinks menu. Before we had all finished ordering we were rejoined by Herr Tapfer. He placed his hand gently on the waiter's shoulder.

"Tear up that order, there's a good chap," he said. "Just fetch us a bottle of your best champagne."

"After all," he explained, as he sat down in the empty seat next to me, "it's Christmas, we have had a good party, I have successfully completed my first term at university and am on my way to a lifetime's ambition, why not celebrate in style, with champagne?"

No one seemed inclined to disagree with him, provided of course he was paying for it.

I had been going through some very strange emotional upheavals over the last twenty minutes or so, ever since we left the party, in fact. Away from the romantic music and the closed unreal atmosphere of the hall I had begun to sober up and the warm feeling of well-being was quickly subsiding into cold feet. It wasn't that I didn't like Chantal - I liked her a lot - but I wanted her as a friend not a girlfriend and I'd got rather more involved this evening than I'd intended or even contemplated. Ironically, after all the romantic fantasies I'd harboured before meeting Chantal for the first time, I'd decided that I didn't really want a girlfriend anyway. I'd grown to like things the way they were, going out in a group on a regular basis, with no ties personally and no relationships within the group. I didn't want anything to spoil that. The problem now was that I didn't have a clue what Chantal was feeling. For me, much as I hated to admit it, the opportunity for a little closeness with a girl just happened to have come at the right time. If I was really truthful I would probably have admitted that it could really have been anyone - well anyone attractive and female that is. Now, if it had been the same for Chantal then there was no problem. On the other hand, if she was genuinely attracted to me and believed I felt the same way then I was in big trouble. Whatever I did was going to hurt her and possibly destroy the relationship of the group as well. As often in the past I wished I could read someone else's mind, just for a moment, so at least I could be sure.

After a few glasses of champagne things didn't seem that bad. Somehow, on taking our places at the table in the bar, we had got separated. I was sandwiched between Herr Tapfer and Ewa and Chantal was next to Mike and De Beauvoir. She was chatting away happily to the Frenchman, laughing and sipping champagne, and seemed to have completely forgotten about me. I tried to catch her eye a few times, wanting somehow to probe in her mind, but without success. Eventually, under the influence of the champagne, I began to feel rather more optimistic and soon convinced myself that everything was alright. After all there were no little hidden glances passing between us, no secret signs, and that was what was supposed to happen if you were moving into some kind of relationship, wasn't it? Obviously, she felt the same way as me. It was fun for a while but nothing serious. She was probably thinking about a boyfriend back in France all the time. Yes, there wouldn't be any problems. We were both adults. I relaxed, drank some more champagne and listened, preening myself, while Ewa and Herr Tapfer told me how wonderfully I spoke German.

I met Mike for lunch the nest day at the usual place.
"Hi, Mike," I said cheerily, "recovered from last night?"
"Yes," he replied coldly.
"Great party, wasn't it?" I ploughed on oblivious.

"It was alright."

"Is something the matter?"

"What do you think?"

I was confused. This wasn't like Mike at all.

"Is it something I've done?"

"Of course it's something you've bloody done," he almost shouted, his face turning red with anger. "You...you...heartless bastard."

I was really worried now. I'd never seen Mike lose his temper and he'd certainly never spoken to me like this before. I racked my brains, desperately trying to think of what I could have done to upset him.

"OK, OK. What have I done?"

"You know well enough," he snarled, "don't play the innocent with me."

That was it. I'd had enough.

"Look mate, either you bloody tell me what this is all about or I'm going now."

"Chantal," he said bitterly. "That's what it's about, Chantal. Name ring a bell does it, or have you forgotten her already?"

The alarm bells started to go off in my head. I'd conveniently pushed any thoughts of Chantal to one side, preferring to believe everything had sorted itself out quite nicely.

"What about Chantal?"

"Well I presume you remember what you did with Chantal at the party?"

"Of course I do. It was very nice but nothing serious."

"Perhaps Chantal didn't see it that way?"

I was beginning to panic now.

"What do you mean? Come on, stop playing twenty questions and tell me what this is all about."

"Alright. We all went home by car last night, yes?"

"Yes."

"We dropped you off first, right?"

"Correct."

"Fine. I was watching you as you said goodbye to Chantal. She was sitting there waiting for you to kiss her, or thank her, or ask to see her again or even just acknowledge that something had happened. And what did you do? You wished a merry goodnight to the world in general, didn't even look at Chantal, and waltzed off into the night totally oblivious. She was hurt for God's sake, almost in tears. She hardly said a word for the rest of the journey, just sat there staring into space." He lost his temper again at the memory. "It was so bloody callous, Iain. It was inhuman."

I was mortified. I hadn't even thought about it at the time. I'd long since convinced myself that, like me, Chantal just wanted to forget about it. The possibility that I'd hurt her made me feel sick inside.

"Oh God," I moaned, "what a mess. I didn't know...I mean I didn't realize...I thought..." I tailed off into incoherence. It was all too much.

"You're not trying to say that you didn't know she'd feel hurt. You must have known. You had your fun and then dropped her as soon as it was over. That's the long and the short of it."

Even in my distressed state I wasn't about to let him wander into the realms of melodrama.

"Oh, come off it. You're trying to make me sound like a second Casanova, love them and leave them and damn their feelings. I didn't seduce her, for God's sake. We had a dance together and it got out of hand. You know I'm not a womaniser. Now cut the self-righteous nonsense and try and help instead."

Mike began to calm down a little.

"Alright, alright. You're not a heartless bastard, just a stupid one. But whether you meant it or not we've still got problems."

"I know, I know. The last thing I want is to upset Chantal, especially just as things were going so well socially. What am I going to do?"

"Well you'll have to sort it out before she goes home on Saturday."

"Too right. I don't want this hanging over me all through Christmas. I'll have to go and talk to her."

The next twenty-four hours were sheer hell. I was dreading talking to Chantal again but I wanted to get it over with as quickly as possible. I skipped lunch that day and went straight round to where she lived but there was nobody in. I went back at four, again at six and eight and then finally back again at ten, each time knocking in vain for long periods. I hardly slept at all that night, tossing and turning in my bed, haunted by images of a distraught, tearful Chantal suffering alone somewhere, hating me. There was a gnawing ache of regret in my stomach and my head hurt so much I thought it would burst. In the end, I got up at dawn and walked over to Chantal's to push a note through her door telling her to contact me as soon as possible. At seven-thirty I went back yet again only to be told by a yawning housemate, still in pyjamas, that she didn't think Chantal had come home at all the night before.

By the time I met Mike at lunchtime I was a wreck, totally sunk in misery and frustration and far too distraught to eat. Seeing me so obviously upset, Mike had tempered his outrage considerably and most of his anger had been diluted by sympathy. But there was very little he could offer in the way of help and advice other than 'keep trying'. And all the time there was the haunting image of Chantal, hurt and wounded, following me wherever I went.

When finally, at six o'clock that evening, on my fifth visit of the day, the door was opened by a bright, cheerful, not at all distraught Chantal, it was a bit of a shock.

"My goodness," she said, "you look absolutely terrible. What on earth's the matter?"

"I need to talk to you," I blurted out. "Can I come in? Please?"

"Of course. Come inside and sit down."

It was an indescribable relief to be able to talk to Chantal at last and I just poured out the whole story from beginning to end. She listened to me in silence until I'd finished and then shook her head sorrowfully.

"I always knew the English were a bit strange," she said, "but this is ridiculous even for them. Fancy getting yourself so worked up over nothing. You are silly Iain."

After all the worry and self-recrimination I couldn't handle this.

"What you mean you weren't upset on Tuesday?"

"Oh, I was upset, yes. Of course I was. But not because I was expecting promises of undying love or anything like that. I haven't fallen desperately in love with you if that's what Mike thought. I just wanted you to acknowledge it had happened, that's all. I mean, it did happen and it was a lovely evening and even if that's all there was to it you could at least have kissed me goodnight. What upset me was you pretending it hadn't even taken place. You were so cold."

That made me feel really guilty. She was absolutely right of course, I'd simply run away from it.

"I really am sorry Chantal," I said, meaning every word. "It was a cowardly and unfeeling thing to do and I'm sorry I hurt you."

"It's OK. No bones broken."

I got up and went over to where she sat and kissed her on the cheek.

"Thank you for a lovely evening," I said. "It was wonderful."

She returned the kiss and smiled.

"Thank you kind sir. It was my pleasure."

"Forgiven?"

"Forgiven."

"Oh good. Mike will be relieved."

I was right. Mike was.

"Well thank God that's over," he said as we sat together later over a beer.

"I was beginning to wonder what would crack up first - you or our social life."

"It was a close run thing but I think we just about averted disaster on both fronts."

"Yes. I think you're right."

"How about you? Have you forgiven me yet?"

"Of course. You've restored the status quo and upheld the tradition of English chivalry. That's good enough for me."

He offered me his hand and assumed a heavy upper-class accent.

"Congratulations, old boy, you're a Gentleman again."

I reached forward and we shook hands laughing. There was still one nagging doubt in my mind, however, and I decided I might as well clear the air completely while I had the chance.

"There's just one more thing," I said, choosing my words as carefully as possible. "Was it just a sense of chivalry that made you so angry yesterday or was there more to it than that?"

He was thoughtful for a moment and then gave me a wry smile.

"Well I suppose there was really," he answered. "You see I'd spent most of the previous day planning to do something of the sort with

Chantal that night, if the opportunity arose, but you got there first. I was as jealous as hell!"

Chapter Nineteen

"That's your idea of off-piste skiing is it?" asked Hans, looking down at me in exasperation. "What did I specifically tell you not to do?"

"Get too close to the edge before turning," I replied sheepishly.

"Exactly. And what did you do?"

"I got too close to the edge."

"Right again. And now just look at you."

I was not a pretty sight. I was half-sitting, half-lying several feet down the slope off the edge of the marked run, my torso buried in soft powder snow and my skis sticking up in the air at an alarming angle.

"How many times do I have to tell you," he continued, "that you are not good enough to make sharp parallel turns on the edge like that? If this had been a narrow pass with a sheer drop on either side instead of these nice soft slopes you would have been dead by now. And what's worse is that I've now got to waste my valuable time getting you out."

It was the Sunday before Christmas and this was my third day's training with Hans. It wasn't getting any easier. His whole personality seemed to change as soon as he put on a pair of skis, transforming him from mild-mannered teacher Hans Reitenberger into Attila the Instructor. Today, for a treat, he'd brought me up to Igls to try the Olympic downhill run on the *Patscherkofel* and, as he'd forecast, I was beginning to wish I'd stayed at home. It was my own fault of course. I'd spent every free day skiing on the *Mutterer Alm* and I'd told him I was bored with it. Also, because it was an extremely easy run, I'd developed a ridiculously inflated view of my own ability and Hans had decided to kill two birds with one stone - take me somewhere new and cut me down to size all at the same time. It was working.

Hans skied down off the edge of the piste and set about helping me back up.

"Right. Well you'll have to take those skis off first otherwise you'll never get out." He leaned over and pulled the catch on the back of the binding on each ski until it clicked up. Then he carefully pulled the skis away from my boots and stuck them in the ground beside him.

"OK, now give me your poles."

I unhooked the ski-poles from round my wrists and handed them over. He stuck them into the ground by the skis.

"Now the difficult bit. Turn yourself round until your feet are pointing downhill and then stand up."

This was a real struggle. The snow was deep and soft and heavy and any movement was tricky. There wasn't much Hans could do to help with his skis on and he just stood watching impatiently as I slowly scrabbled through the thick blanket and finally managed to stand up. The snow was up to my knees.

"I should really make you put those skis back on and side-step up," he said, "but it's Christmas at the end of the week and I'd rather like to be at home for it. Carry them and walk up."

He side-stepped easily back up to the piste and then waited again as I plodded heavily through the thick powder. Eventually, red-faced and panting, I struggled back onto the slope. I laid the skis down resting against Hans' feet so they wouldn't slip and he used his ski-pole to knock the snow off each of my boots in turn so that I could put the skis back on. At last I was ready again and he looked at me sternly.

"We have just wasted almost twenty minutes there, all because you didn't do as you were told. We're going to continue on down this narrower bit doing parallels and you're going to turn exactly where I tell you to. If you go over the edge again I shall leave you there. Is that clear?"

I nodded chastened. I didn't want to go through all that again.

Despite the fact that it was an Olympic slope, it wasn't as difficult as I'd imagined. Hans had chosen a day when the snow was soft and easy and, by the time we'd arrived, most of the early morning ice had disappeared. On race days water was poured down the slope to turn it into a solid sheet of ice and that was when it became treacherous and a challenge for the world-class skiers. On my own, abandoning any pretence of style, I could probably have got down it like this without too many mishaps. On easy snow, it was always possible to slither down sideways or inch your way down in the snowplough position. But Hans was only interested in doing it properly.

"Any holiday skier can do that," he'd said at one point. "You don't need much skill to side-slip down a narrow pass in this sort of snow. But if that's how you want to ski then I'll stop wasting my time and leave you to it."

So properly was how we did it. Neat parallel turns from side to side through the pass until we came out of the trees and onto a wider, bumpier terrain.

"OK," said Hans, stopping sideways in a flurry of snow, "that wasn't too bad. But watch that left leg when you're turning left. It's lazy and it doesn't always come round parallel. You need to practice that on your own. We're going to try something a bit different now." He pointed at the slope ahead. "That's a mogul field. The moguls are those bumps you can see. I'll teach you how to cross them. This is not a very difficult one but it's a good place to start."

I didn't like the look of the moguls. They made any of the skiing I'd done so far seem like a gentle walk.

"We'll only try this once for today because it's hard work on the legs. I want you to stand here and watch me go down, concentrating on the way I turn between the bumps. Then I'll watch you come down from the bottom. Alright?"

I nodded and he set off, twisting and turning elegantly round the moguls, skis parallel, in an almost straight line to the bottom. Then he signalled for me to follow.

I could see how he'd done it but I just couldn't do it myself. The idea seemed to be that you avoided the moguls and skied between them instead, turning on the narrow, flat ground joining them together. It looked simple but in practice it was horrendously difficult. The gaps were narrow, steep and often bumpy as well. Sometimes, as you came to turn, there was no real gap at all and I kept ending up balanced precariously on the side or the top of a mogul, necessitating a lot of work with my poles to slide back down again. In the end, I was afraid to turn at all, traversing right to the edge of the mogul field in a convenient rut before I had no choice but to jump round and hope. It took me ages to get down and I was a broken man by the time I rejoined Hans.

"Well, I made a right mess of that," I said sheepishly, waiting for the torrent of criticism. But this time none came.

"No. It wasn't too bad for a first attempt. It's a difficult technique to master and it needs time."

He could see that I'd been expecting him to be harder.

"I don't expect you to be an expert first time, you know," he said, patting me on the shoulder. "I just expect you to try your best and do as you're told, that's all. I only get annoyed when you don't listen."

As usual, we finished off with a long run down and Hans took it a lot faster than he'd done the previous two times up on the Mutterer Alm. I had a real job trying to keep up with him but just managed to hang in behind him until the last few hundred metres when he dropped into a crouch, tucked his sticks under his arms and his hands together under his chin and *schüssed* the rest of the way leaving me standing. By the time I reached him, he already had his skis off and was tying them together with a thick rubber clasp.

"You're improving," he said as I took off my skis, "but discipline is still your biggest problem. You've got to do it the right way every time, not just when I'm watching. If you ski any old how when you're on your own you'll never really be any good. The same goes for doing as you're told. When I tell you something it's because years of experience, mine and other people's, have proved that it works. It's not just some theory you can take or leave, we're talking about life and death up there."

"I know. I'm sorry Hans. I never was any good at being told what to do. That's why I keep failing my driving test."

He laughed.

"How many times is it?"

"Four so far."

"Well up on a ski slope you might not get four chances. Just remember that."

"I will."

We picked up the skis and started to walk back to the car.

"You can forget Mutters now," he said, "and come up here and practice instead. It's easier to get to on your own and there's a lot more variety. Practice that mogul run. It'll do you good."

He was certainly right about it being easier to get to. Without a car, Innsbruck wasn't actually the best place to go skiing from, compared to the real ski resorts, for example, although it certainly had the edge over Hertfordshire. Both Mutters and Igls required a tram journey across town and then a ride by mountain tram up into the villages. Mutters was further out and also required a long walk from the tram stop in heavy, uncomfortable boots while carrying skis. I invariably came back on my day-off with blisters. Not only was Igls nearer but the Patscherkofel cable car was also easier to get to.

"If you practice hard," continued Hans, "you might even be able to ski with the bottom class when you go to ski camp."

I smiled quietly. This was obviously just a ploy to make me practice. Of course I'd be good enough to ski with at least the bottom class.

He caught the smile.

"You think I'm joking don't you. Well I promise you I'm not. We work at a ski-camp in exactly the same way they do on skiing holidays. All the kids do a ski past on the first day, one by one, and we grade them into six or seven different classes. The difference is that even our bottom class is often way better than the top class on a skiing holiday. These kids have been skiing since they were five, most of them, and the ones from the high villages live on skis during the winter. They're all experts by your standards. The top class can even have potential Olympic champions in it. Take young Lizzi Bauer in 7d, she's already junior national slalom champion and could be a Gold-medallist one day. If you make it into the bottom class it will be a real achievement but don't bank on it. It'll be tough. And even then you'll be bottom of the bottom class."

That wiped the smile off my face. It was obvious when I thought about it but, as usual, I hadn't thought.

"What happens if I'm not good enough?" I asked him.

"No problem. You just ski on your own like you do on your days off. We seriously wouldn't put you in a class if you weren't good enough. It wouldn't be fair on the others. You'd hold them up. But don't worry about it. The assistants never normally ski with a class unless they're from skiing countries like Scotland or Canada and have skied a lot before.

"And which class will you be leading?"

"The top class, of course," he answered with a smile, "so you definitely won't be with me. But you go out and practice as much as you can. I would really like to see you get into that bottom class. It would be just like Pygmalion."

"Alright, Professor Higgins," I said, "I'll do my best."

And I meant it, too.

Back home that evening I set about packing my suitcase. On Wednesday, I would be leaving Innsbruck for England and Christmas with my family. Chantal had left the day before and she'd dropped a Christmas card through my letter box early in the morning on her way to the station with a little ironic note promising me her undying love and saying that she didn't know how she would survive until 'our hearts were once again joined as one'. I'd deserved that, I suppose, and I was pleased that she was treating the whole thing as one big joke. Mike and I had said goodbye to Helga and Lisa the previous evening over an expensive dinner in *Tabasco* and we were now just impatient to get through the last three days of school and be on our way. Not that we had any burning desire to leave Innsbruck. We'd both grown to love the place and the people after the initial ups and downs and we were looking forward to spending the next eight months there. It was just the right time to go back and see our families and friends, take a break from the routine of teaching and tell everyone what a wonderful time we were having. And anyway it was a long journey and I for one just wanted to get it over with.

I was just laying out my Christmas presents in the bottom of the suitcase when the phone rang and I heard Herbie answer it. A few seconds later there was a knock on the door and Herbie called:

"Phone call for you, Iain. It's a Dr. Ziller from your school."

I was rather surprised. Konrad Ziller was the Head of the History Department and a close friend of Reiner's. I knew him reasonably well but it was unusual for him to be ringing me at home, especially on a Sunday night. I had a sudden panic that something might have happened to Reiner.

"Thanks Herbie, I'll come and take it," I called back and rushed out to the phone in the hallway.

"Hello, Konrad, what's the matter?"

"Hi, Iain," said the voice at the other end, "sorry to disturb you at home. I've been trying to ring you all weekend. It's about Willi's thesis. It's been rejected by the Faculty Board on the grounds that the English is too full of mistakes. He has to resubmit a corrected version by Christmas or he fails. Could you possibly come over and give him a hand?"

"But that's impossible Konrad," I said in disbelief. "I checked it before it was submitted. It was excellent."

"Well the board was quite firm about it. We've got a list of their criticisms here."

"I'll be right over. It's nonsense. I'm not having that. See you in twenty minutes." I slammed the phone down, furious.

Thesis correction was another profitable sideline for English speakers in Austria. Unlike England, any thesis for a Doctorate in a foreign language had to be written in the language itself, no matter what the topic was, and it was an accepted practice that all such theses were read and corrected by native speakers if the student could afford it. It was an arduous and often boring job but it paid well and I'd done several in the last couple of months including Willi Ziller's. I'd done that one for nothing, though, since Konrad was both a colleague and a friend of Reiner's. I could see them now wishing they'd paid me to do it, probably feeling that I'd put less effort into it because it was free. But it wasn't true. I'd worked harder on that one than on any of them. For a start, I liked Konrad and Willi, for another thing I knew how much it meant to him because he had a teaching post in the faculty resting on the outcome and his wife was pregnant so he needed the job, but most of all the thesis was brilliant and I'd felt privileged to have had the chance of working on it. I'd sweated blood over it, correcting and polishing the English until I felt it was perfect. I was damned if I was going to let a bunch of foreign professors tell me I couldn't speak English.

By the time I got to Konrad's house, I'd worked myself up into a fine state of indignant anger. As he opened the door I hardly gave him a chance to speak before launching myself into a tirade against the English faculty.

"I guarantee you," I finished as he closed the door behind me, "that the English in that thesis was perfect and I'll go and tell them that myself if necessary."

He led me into the lounge where I found Hans and Reiner drinking wine and talking to Frau Ziller.

"What are you two doing here?" I asked in astonishment.

"Reinforcements," said Reiner, "to see if we can help you get it right this time."

I could feel the fury boiling up inside me. I was beginning to take this whole thing personally. I managed to stop myself biting his head off and sat down and accepted a drink instead.

"Where's Willi?" I asked.

"He's just coming," answered Konrad, sitting down. "He shouldn't be a moment."

"He's probably just trying to find three strong men to help him carry the list of criticisms," said Reiner, risking his life again.

The door opened and in came Willi and his wife Karin, their arms full of reams and reams of paper.

"Right," said Willi, looking very serious, "I've got the corrections here. I'll hand out a chunk to each of you and we can start going through them."

He pulled a fat wad off the top and handed it to Karin.

"Here, give the first one to Iain."

Then suddenly his face broke and he and Karin were convulsed in fits of laughter, joined shortly afterwards by Reiner and everyone else in the room. They were soon hysterical and the piles of paper flew everywhere as they grabbed their aching sides and leant against the door for support.

"Has the whole world gone mad, or what?" I asked totally bewildered. Karin still laughing, came over and slipped her arms round me.

"Poor Iain," she said, between gasps of laughter, "we're so cruel." She recovered herself a little and wiped her eyes with her handkerchief. "It's a joke you see. A practical joke. Willi got the letter yesterday. His thesis has been accepted and he's got the job at the University."

"They say it's one of the best they've seen for years," added Konrad, also pulling himself together. "We wanted to thank you for your invaluable help."

"You've got a funny way of saying thank you over here, that's all I can say."

I was slowly calming down after all the righteous indignation and soon I was laughing with them at the joke at my expense.

"I bet I know whose idea it was, too," I said to Konrad, looking meaningfully at Reiner across the room. "It's got his hallmark stamped all over it."

"I cannot tell a lie," said Reiner, totally unabashed, "it was I." He smiled mischievously. "But you've got to admit it was a bloody good joke."

Grudgingly I had to admit that it was.

We carried on drinking wine for a while, toasting Willi's success and his new job until Konrad put down his glass and called for silence. "Now, to show our thanks properly, we have a little gift for you," he said to me.

"But Konrad, I told you I wouldn't take anything from a colleague," I answered.

"Well we knew you wouldn't accept money," said Willi, "so we thought of something else instead. Just hang on."

He left the room for a few moments and then came back in carrying a magnificent pair of skis.

"For you," he said. "Hans reckons you'll make good use of them while you're here. He came with us to choose them."

I was speechless. They were quality Kneissl skis complete with poles and bindings.

"The boots you'll need to buy yourself," said Hans, "to get the fitting right."

I didn't really know how to thank them. The generosity was overwhelming.

"Thank you. Thank you all very much. But it's crazy. It must have cost you more than simply paying someone else to read the thesis."

"Not at all," said Konrad. "They're last year's model, you see. Someone had used them for a season and then traded them back into the shop for a new pair. Some people change their skis every year to keep up with the new fashions. And the bindings we had already. Hans

213

put them together in his workshop, waxed them and sharpened the edges. They're as good as new."

To me, they were better than new. Not only were they my own skis but they were also a present from friends in Austria so they would always have sentimental value as well. One thing still puzzled me, though.

"You must have known all about this, this morning," I said to Hans. "Why didn't you give me the story about the thesis then to make sure I was free tonight?"

"Well, for a start," he replied, "I asked you when I rang on Friday what your plans were for today and you said you were spending the evening packing. And I confirmed it this morning while we were skiing."

"But more importantly," added Reiner, "I knew you'd flip your lid when we told you the faculty board had criticised your English. I didn't want you to have too long to brood over it. After all I've spent months training you, poor basic material though you are, to be a halfway decent assistant. I didn't want you to have a heart attack and get shipped home for Christmas in a wooden box."

"Thanks for being so considerate," I said ironically. "Anyway what training have you ever given me?"

"Well I like that. Who taught you to play Colonel Puff and pee in the Palace Gardens?"

"Alright," I answered, laughing, "you did."

"Exactly. I wanted to protect my investment."

The party wound up about midnight and Hans drove me home with my skis.

"I'll have to fit your boots to the new bindings before you can use them," said Hans, as he left me at the door, "so if you want to ski as soon as you come back you'll have to use the ones I lent you."

"Thanks. Maybe we could go and get some boots straight after Christmas?"

"Sure. The sooner you get your own boots the better. You really need a pair moulded for your own feet to get the best out of them."

"And thanks for choosing the skis and setting them up."

214

"It was nothing. Just make good use of them, that's all the thanks I want. See you at school tomorrow."

He got back in the car and drove off through the snow.

Inside the flat, I bumped into Rolf, obviously drunk, reeling back from the bathroom. The noise of music and laughter coming from his room was indescribable.

"Hey, Iain," he slurred, slapping me on the back, "have you just been skiing?"

He was clearly drunker than I'd thought.

"No Rolf," I told him, "they were a present from some friends."

"Ah. A Christmas present?"

"Something like that." It was too difficult to explain.

"We're having a party. Come and join us."

I looked at my watch and thought about school at eight o'clock the next morning. Then I listened to the noise and realised I had no chance of getting any sleep anyway. What the hell. After all it was nearly Christmas.

The next two days seemed to drag on forever. I was like a child wishing the time away until Christmas, counting every minute. I packed and repacked my suitcase at least a dozen times and whiled away the rest of the hours when I wasn't at school either eating and drinking too much with Mike or finding still more things to buy that I couldn't possibly go home without, necessitating further repacking of the suitcase. And, then, just as I was beginning to think it was never going to arrive, it was suddenly Wednesday and the start of the holiday for Mike and me.

We both had to work through the morning but I for one was quite glad to be occupied. The train to Munich didn't leave until four and I didn't fancy just waiting around all day with nothing to do. And anyway the end of term atmosphere was contagious. Most of the real work had finished on the Tuesday and the kids were allowed to relax a little for the last two days. I played games with all of my classes and, for a change, they were allowed to speak German to me and teach me some Austrian games. The only exception was, of course, my one lesson with Reiner. The most he would do was to let me spend fifteen minutes playing 'hangman' with his class. When I tentatively suggested allowing them to teach me a game, like the other groups, he just laughed.

"You already know how to play Colonel Puff," he said. "There aren't any other Austrian games worth knowing."

The morning ended with Kristine's first year class, the one I'd hopelessly confused a few weeks before. Their English wasn't good enough for anything but the most basic of games such as, 'I Spy', but they thoroughly enjoyed teaching me games in German and, even more, being able to talk to me in a language that they knew so much better than I ever would. The tables were turned for once and I was the one needing help with difficult vocabulary. Near the end of the lesson Kristine called for silence and turned to me.

"Right. Now we have a special Christmas surprise for you. We've been practising in secret for weeks, haven't we children?"

The buzz of excited chatter confirmed that they had. She quietened them down again and then produced a tuning fork. She tapped it on the desk letting the tone ring out into the room.

"Ok, children, after three. One, two, three."

Hesitantly at first and then with growing confidence they began to sing 'Silent Night' in English. It was beautiful. It was one of my favourite carols anyway, but sung there quietly, without music, especially for my benefit, it was more moving than it had ever been. It was a German carol so they would have been familiar with the tune but they must have put a lot of effort into learning the English words and I was touched. I sat there at the front of the class just letting the music wash over me, the feeling of Christmas growing stronger with each verse. It was the perfect end to my first term at school and the perfect beginning to my Christmas holiday.

After the seemingly endless round of 'goodbye', 'Merry Christmas' and 'see you next year' in the staff room, I went back to the flat and went through the same routine with Herbie, Ingrid and Rolf, who were still my only flatmates. The room next to mine was still vacant. The female medical student who had been due to move in had, in fact, been Herbie's girlfriend of the time or, at least, the main one. They had broken up just before she was supposed to move and it suddenly hadn't seemed like such a good idea after all. A new girl, a pharmacy student, was now joining us in January. I'd been introduced briefly on one occasion and she seemed nice enough. Neither Ingrid nor I had been able to ascertain whether she was another girlfriend or not. Herbie went through them so fast it was difficult to tell.

It was already gone two o'clock when I met Mike, case in hand, in the Old Town.

"Hi," he said, "all ready?"

"As I'll ever be," I replied, thankfully dropping the case for a while to rest my arm. "Are we going to eat?"

"I think we'd better. We won't get another chance till Munich and that's hours away."

"Well the *Mensa* is shut now so it'll have to be a restaurant. How about the *Wurschtkessel*? That serves all day and it's on the way to the station."

"That'll do. I like their goulash."

Wurschtkessel was one of the many restaurants we'd got to know once we started to get paid regularly. It served mainly local specialities and the food was good and cheap. It was very popular with the tourists and was one of the few places that treated them like human beings. We'd learnt most of what we knew about local food from there and from the waitress at the '*Löwe*'. There was a noticeable lack of patience among the staff at most of the other places when it came to explaining dishes on the menu.

Mike's appetite was as healthy as ever but I made do with a snack.

"What's the matter?" he asked tucking into a plate of goulash and potatoes, "You not hungry?"

"I never eat much when I'm travelling," I answered. "I just go into a sort of limbo until it's over."

"What you mean you dance under doors all the way?"

For a change, I gave him one of my withering looks but it had even less effect than one of his on me.

"Because if that's what you're planning," he continued, "I'm travelling in a different compartment. I'm not having the sound of primitive jungle rhythms keeping me awake all night."

"Finished?"

"Yes, I think so."

"Good. Let me rephrase that. I don't like travelling particularly so my body shuts down for the duration. Is that better?"

"Infinitely. Anyway I thought you liked travelling?"

"I like being in different places. I don't much like getting to them. And this train journey's going to be murder.

"Oh, come on, it won't be that bad."

"It will, I guarantee you. I've done the same sort of journey back from the South of France. It's too hot, too cramped and boring as hell. And it's Christmas. From Munich to Ostend that train's going to be a cattle truck."

Mike shrugged

"We'll be alright," he said confidently. "The train starts at Munich so we'll just have to get on early and grab a compartment. It'll be fun travelling across Europe by train. It was alright on the way out to Vienna."

"Yes, but we were all travelling as a group in our own coach. This time it's just us and the rest of the world."

Mike wasn't convinced.

"Well I intend to enjoy it, even if you don't. It's part of the holiday as far as I'm concerned."

"I just hope that, by some miracle, I can sleep all the way."

"You're still looking forward to getting home though aren't you?"

"Of course. Wild horses wouldn't stop me."

"It's going to be strange being back though," he continued, thoughtfully. "I'm not used to speaking English in shops and things any more. I'll keep breaking into German. They'll think I'm mad in rural Kent."

"They'll probably think you're a spy or something. You'll have Special Branch watching the house for three weeks.

"It'll be really weird feeling like a foreigner in your own country. I wonder if people will think we've changed."

"We must have changed a bit. You can't go through an experience like this and not come out of it a bit different."

"Yes," Mike said ironically, "like the grey hairs and the worry lines."

"Oh, it was a bit rough at first but I wouldn't swap it now."

"Neither would I. It's a great place to live and it's been really good the last month or so. I'm glad this is not the end. It'd be awful not to be coming back."

I agreed. I was already dreading doing this journey at the end of the year. I'd thought a lot about what Bud had said on my second day in Innsbruck, over the last week, and I now understood what he'd meant about looking back on that day and wishing I could go through it all over again. Of course I didn't feel like that now. Things had just started to sort themselves out and the best was still to come in the next two terms. But at the end of the year I knew I'd be wishing exactly that and I was already wondering whether I'd ever want to leave for good.

At three-thirty we were back where it had all begun, standing in the entrance at Innsbruck main station waiting to board the Munich train on the first leg of the journey back to England. It felt strange to be leaving Innsbruck. With the exception of the painful day trip to Italy, it was the first time I had been out of the town and the surrounding area in three months. In that time, it had become home, almost as familiar to me as the town in which I was born. I couldn't imagine how I would feel when I came back after Christmas, whether I would feel homesick again or not. But I couldn't believe I would ever feel like a stranger there again. I'd given up a part of me that was English and replaced it with something that was Austrian and I didn't think that was something I would ever lose. I was leaving a foreign town I'd grown to know well for a familiar town I'd grown away from. For three weeks, I would be caught between the two, the return to Innsbruck ever present in my mind, stopping me settling back completely into my real home again. And that was why the journey was so special. As we set off to board the train I was filled with a sense of excitement and well-being. I was going home, back to my family and friends for a Christmas that I confidently expected to be one of the best I'd ever had, but at the end of it all there was Innsbruck again, with all my new friends, all my pupils and all the places I'd grown to love.

It was a glorious prospect.